Some Theological Reflections

What Did Jesus Do?

WILLIAM EMMANUEL ABRAHAM

WestBow Press books may be ordered through booksellers or by contacting:

WestBow Press
A Division of Thomas Nelson & Zondervan
1663 Liberty Drive
Bloomington, IN 47403
www.westbowpress.com
1 (866) 928-1240

ISBN: 978-1-5127-8562-3 (sc)
ISBN: 978-1-5127-8563-0 (hc)
ISBN: 978-1-5127-8561-6 (e)

Library of Congress Control Number: 2017907203

Print information available on the last page.

WestBow Press rev. date: 05/22/2017

Contents

Acknowledgments

I wish to thank for their forbearance all members of my family, my friends, and my co-parishioners on whom I inflicted earlier versions of this work. In particular, I express my deepest appreciation to my wife, Marya, for the uncomplaining effort that she put into nursing and proofing all those interminable versions, and for her quiet encouragement.

Above all, I must mention my son, Henry Abraham; John Lucken, who not only rewrote and greatly improved the introduction but also cogently suggested an endpoint for the text; John Huntriss, who subjected a preceding version to trenchant criticism and must accept some responsibility for changes in the present version; my fellow usher in church, Stephen Tauhouse, who frequently discussed my interpretations; and, last, my longtime friend, Distinguished Professor Emeritus Kwasi Wiredu, all of whom, at various times and by diverse hints, planted in my mind the idea of seeking publication.

Blame them.

WEA

INTRODUCTION

Caiaphas's decision that Jesus be sacrificed as a ransom for the Jewish nation (and, according to Jesus, also for the Gentile nations) set in motion events that would lead to the crucifixion. There were strict laws and protocols governing sacrifices to God, and had the sacrifice of Jesus not observed all the relevant laws, the entire sacrifice would have been invalid. In that case, neither Caiaphas himself, nor Jesus's apostles, nor the Jewish people, would have been able to accept the slaying as a sacrifice rather than sheer murder. So any account of Jesus's sacrifice must show proper adherence to those laws and protocols.

Two basic prerequisites in any sacrifice were that the designated victim carry a seal of approval, given by a priest to certify that it was spotless and without blemish, and that the slaying itself be validly carried out.

In the case of Jesus's sacrifice, Peter addressed both points. Spotlessness in a human being would be not only physical but also moral and spiritual. The Father himself had placed the seal of approval on Jesus, and Peter dwelt on this spotlessness in his own statement that Jesus had committed no sin, nor did he ever utter an untruth, thus making him fit to bear our sins in his own person to the cross (1 Peter 2:22–24). That very same spotlessness would be required of Jesus in order to act as officiating priest without a prior, and arguably futile, self-cleansing ritual.

It is the stringency of this requirement of sinlessness that more or less gives rise to chapter 2, on the necessity of the immaculate conception and the virgin birth, which together enabled Jesus to be both high priest and sacrificial victim.

Peter also addressed the legal validity of Jesus's slaying. This was rather complex, since human sacrifice was prohibited under Judaic Law, yet Caiaphas had suggested Jesus as a sacrifice for the Jewish nation. As Jesus himself predicted, and Caiaphas and his Sanhedrin came to see (Matthew 26:1), there was only one way in which Jesus could be validly slain, causing Peter to say "This man, handed over to you according to the definite plan and foreknowledge of God, you crucified and killed by the hands of those outside the law" (Acts 2:23 NRSV). The legal issues involved are fully discussed in chapter 8, on the reason for the Gentile involvement in the crucifixion.

One benefit of proceeding this way is the greatly reduced need to resort to metaphysical creations as a way to understand the various phases of what Jesus did; for example, by strictly adhering to the Law, we are led to an understanding of how Jesus could offer his flesh and blood for consumption in a land where that would have been an abomination (pages 39–46).

Chapter 1

The Expectation of Restoration

Messianic expectation always looked to a king who would be descended from David, one whose throne, like David's, would last forever (2 Samuel 7:16). However, Deuteronomy 18:15 had Moses prophesying to the Israelites that God would in future raise up from among them and their own kinsmen a prophet like himself. This prophet they were to be sure to heed. In fact, it was this particular prediction that gave rise to several additional expectations of the Messiah, depending on the particular dominant feature of Moses found most arresting. Accordingly, those who saw Moses as a teacher of righteousness, on account of the Ten Commandments and his other precepts, expected the Messiah to be, like Moses himself, a teacher of righteousness and, in Moses's own words, a prophet. He would give utterance to the mind of God. He would proclaim God's will to the people and their leaders, and he would see them in the manner that God himself sees them.

On the other hand, people who saw Moses principally as the liberator of the Israelites from the yoke of Pharaoh would come to look on the Messiah as a conqueror who would liberate the people from imperial shackles and restore the kingdom to Israel. Those who saw Moses as the founder of the Aaronic priesthood, and himself a priest (Psalm 99:6), would expect the Messiah to be likewise a priest of God—one whose priesthood, like Moses's own priesthood, would not flow from human anointing. The expected

Messiah would guide the people in proper worship and intervene with God on their behalf.

Although Jesus did come as king, the leaders of the Judean people generally had little inkling of his proper dignity. In contrast with the leaders, ordinary individuals and crowds had much more than that: like Nathaniel, who, on first meeting Jesus, proclaimed him to be the Son of God and the King of Israel (John 1:49); like Martha, who also declared her belief that Jesus was the Christ, the Son of God (John 11:27); like the sundry crowds who on diverse occasions attempted to proclaim Jesus king (John 6:15), and who, on the occasion of his entry into Jerusalem on a donkey, in fact did so with their knowing exclamation: "Hosanna! Blessed is the one who comes in the name of the Lord—the King of Israel!" (John 12:13 NRSV; cf Luke 19:38). All of those declarations were indeed acknowledgements of Jesus's dignity, acknowledgments commencing better than three decades earlier with the confession of the Magi, who knew Jesus as the one born king of Israel (Matthew 2:2), and who brought with them gifts customary for kings and deities.

In hopes that Jesus was indeed the longed-for deliverer, a tantalized but expectant audience gathered around him on the timely occasion of the commemoration of the rededication and reconsecration of the Holy temple by the Maccabees, and demanded to know how long he intended to keep them in suspense. They adjured him to say whether he was indeed the Christ (John 10:22–24).

At the same time, Jesus's own generally pacific temperament and his self-submerging ethical teachings had fostered a quandary even among his disciples. Though his teachings and his very temperament were not at all consonant with familiar models of Judean conquering heroes, such as Samson or David, he was certainly perceived to possess power. Had not his disciples watched him overwhelm demons and suppress billows of the sea? Consequently, they generally harbored wistful hopes that it would surely be he who would liberate the nation. His apostles deemed the period of his final journey to Jerusalem to be a most appropriate occasion to do so. They asked him again whether the time was not right for him to restore the kingdom to the nation. After the resurrection, his own uncle, Cleophas (sometimes Cleopas), while on the way to Emmaus, ruefully complained to the resurrected but unrecognized Jesus that they had hoped that Jesus would be the one to restore the kingdom, but he had instead got himself crucified by the Romans. Even moments before his ascension, Jesus was still being desperately asked whether the time had not finally arrived for him to restore the kingdom to the nation.

As long ago as the Babylonian exile, Ezekiel 36:8–11 and Isaiah 60:1–7 had prophesied that the Lord would return the people of Judah and Israel to their own land, and unite them under one Davidic king. Yahweh himself would return and dwell among them in a rebuilt and rededicated Jerusalem temple, just as he had done in the first temple built under Solomon. The physical temple was indeed rebuilt in 515 BC, but eventually underwent an extensive transformation under Herod the Great. Yahweh would take back Mother Zion, whom he had divorced for her infidelity, and denounced as barren and widowed. Judah was in time rejuvenated. Her formerly estranged husband, God, in due course fathered Jesus on the body of Judah. Those disciples who discerned in Jesus the completer of the restoration prophecy naturally expected that he would in short order expel the Roman interlopers.

Meanwhile, until the appearance of the awaited Davidic king, civil authority was to lie in the hands of the high priest. At any time that the Davidic king was properly recognized, the high priest would cede all civil authority to him. So in Jesus's day, the high priest would announce to the Roman proconsul that the Judean nation now had its own king, and really had no need of Caesar's suzerainty. At the time of Jesus's arrest, the high priest Caiaphas had little doubt that any such declaration would elicit from Pontius Pilate, a man who was given to teaching painful lessons, nothing short of devastation upon the nation. That would be an eventuality far from a reestablished kingdom. For this reason, Caiaphas resisted the increasingly popular clamor that Jesus be anointed king (Luke 19:38, John 6:15), and insisted that it would be better to sacrifice Jesus (who was after all only one person) in order to safeguard the nation. When seen in this light, the heretical protestation before the procurator, Pontius Pilate, which his chief priests and their Sadducee advisers instigated ("We have no king but Caesar!") would appear to have been not so much a sycophantic confession as a sagacious and deliberate subordination of prophecy to statecraft. In his own sermons and teachings, Jesus indicated that with him the kingdom of heaven was at hand and indeed already present, thereby identifying himself as the Messiah (Matthew 3:2, 4:17). When he confirmed before the high priest that he was indeed the Messiah, the Sanhedrin passed that claim on to the Roman administration, but hardly in the right spirit.

Jesus did come as prophet. As the role of prophet matured, the prophet came to simulate the conscience of God among the people. He was to utter terrible condemnation for moral and religious aberrations, and yet declare God's compassion—all the while promising to avert a terrible future through confession, repentance, and conversion. The prophet was, at the same time, the people's advocate before God, invoking God's mercy and compassion on their behalf. In exilic and postexilic times, the role of the prophet underwent its final change, and now became principally concerned with the hope of Israel's restored fortunes. It was in this milieu that John the Baptist arrived, the prophet voice of one crying in the wilderness. He exhorted the people to prepare the way of the saving Lord, for whose recognition he had been given identifying clues (John 1:33–34).

Jesus definitively declared God's will, and his authority to do so was confirmed by the astounding miracles that he performed by the Spirit of God (Matthew 12:28, cf Acts 2:22). He taught that it was God's will to be worshipped in spirit and in truth, and he clarified the heart of the law by combining Deuteronomy 6:5 with Leviticus 19:18. We are to love the Lord our God with all our hearts, and with all our souls, and with all our strength, and with our entire minds (Deuteronomy 6:5, Mark 12:30, Matthew 22:37, Luke 10:27). In addition, we are to love our neighbors as ourselves (Leviticus 19:18, Matthew 22:39, Mark 12:31, Luke 10:27). Doing this would require us to live not by a legalistic and minimalist acquiescence, but by deeds and attitudes of supererogation in the spirit of the Sermon on the Plain (Luke 6:27–49).

Chapter 2

The Necessity of the Immaculate Conception and the Virgin Birth to Jesus as High Priest and Victim

Jesus did come as High Priest. It is true that the priesthood established by Moses was intended to devolve from Aaron through his male successors, or generally through his family in the absence of a direct male successor. However, not all those who were properly recognized as priests in Tanakh (the Hebrew Bible) were descendants of Aaron. No less an authority than the Psalms declared Moses to have been a priest of God (Psalm 99:6 NRSV): "Moses and Aaron were among his priests." How, indeed, could it have been otherwise with Moses, the man who anointed and consecrated Aaron himself and his sons as well, the man who sprinkled ritual blood on the altar, the man who was Israel's first intermediary with God, the one who delivered the tablets of the Law to them, the one whose interventions with God secured forgiveness and forestalled their utter annihilation in the desert? Neither Aaron himself nor any of his successors had greater *priestly* accomplishments than those.

Even Gentiles were to produce priests. At Isaiah 66:18, 21, God announces that he will gather all nations and tongues and out of those Gentiles he will take priests and Levites!

It is actually inconsequential that Moses never offered a sacrifice for the transgressions of the people. In fact only one such sacrifice would in the end be successful, that of Jesus, the Lamb of God, of which all intended atonement sacrifices would be intimations. Even though God spoke of sacrifices as peace offerings, apparently he never asked the people for an atonement sacrifice (Jeremiah 7:22). Such sacrifices were in fact priestly accretions on the Ten Commandments. With regard to sins, God had only asked for repentance, as John the Baptist was in his time to proclaim. As to the innumerable sacrifices for sin, God even declared himself weary of them (Isaiah 1:11).

In any case, it is not as if the Aaronic priesthood would have borne much relevance to Jesus's particular mission—to free the human race from everlasting death. That mission would have presented the Aaronic priesthood with insurmountable difficulties, were it to have fallen within its provenance, since no male human being begotten of human parents can himself be without sin. As Paul has it in Romans 3:10 (NRSV), "There is no one who is righteous, not even one" and "all have sinned, and fall short of the glory of God" (3:23 NRSV); Psalms 14:3 (NRSV): "They have all gone astray, they are all alike perverse; there is no one who does good, no, not one." Psalm 143:2 (NRSV): "Do not enter into judgment with your servant, for no one living is righteous before you." Indeed, Psalm 53:2–3 (NRSV): "God looks down from heaven on humankind to see if there are any who are wise, who seek after God. They have all fallen away, they are all alike perverse; there is no one who does good, no, not one." Also, Ecclesiastes 7:20 (NRSV): "Surely, there is no one on earth so righteous as to do good without ever sinning"; and 1 John 1:8 (NRSV): "If we say that we have no sin, we do deceive ourselves and the truth is not in us." As Jesus himself put it at Matthew 19:17, no one is good but God alone.

Yet, by protocol, a person who is encumbered with sin cannot offer a sacrifice to God for the sins of the people. It was indeed for this reason that the high priest, on whom that duty fell, was required to offer a sacrifice for his own sins before presuming to offer the same for the sins of the people. In addition, for that sacrifice to be efficacious, its victim, too, had to be without blemish.

It goes without saying, however, that every sacrificial animal, be it ever so spotless, still undergoes a forcible and involuntary death. While this process may satisfy the *form* of a sacrifice, it probably cannot meet the *material* requirements of one. The consent of the victim would appear to be indispensable to the proper consummation of a sacrifice. Even though it is an extraordinarily virtuous deed to offer one's own life for another's, offering a third party as a nonvoluntary victim would hardly seem satisfactory. This should mean that the high priest's sacrifice for his own sins, as well as his sacrifices of further animals for the sins of the people, could only have met the formal, but not the material, requirements of a sacrifice for sin, since the animal victims' deaths would in every case have been involuntary.

Clearly, the offering of even a prized animal or other immensely valuable possession would fall short as a sacrifice. What, indeed, could a person offer for the redemption of his own life or soul, as Jesus pointedly asked (Matthew 16:26, Mark 8:37). The need for a free choice, one not made under duress or in consequence of any other inducement, is precisely what Jesus was stressing in declaring that in his own case his own self-sacrifice for the sins of the whole world would be free, and not compelled by anyone else. Sacrifice under duress or other constraint is no sacrifice. As a consequence, this must mean that no Aaronic high priest would be able to conduct a sacrifice for sin that would be satisfactory in all respects, whether for his own sins or for the sins of others.

This should naturally bring up the question of what is required of a human being who is intended as a sacrificial victim for the sins of the whole world. Just as the animal victims had to be spotless, so would the human victim have to be spotless, though not in the manner of an animal, but in a human way and in every human dimension—physical, moral, and spiritual. Truly, it would be easy enough for a human being begotten of human parents to be physically spotless. However, moral and spiritual spotlessness would be quite another matter altogether. Since, as we have seen the Bible say, no one born of human parents is morally and spiritually spotless, a satisfactory expiating human victim should not have been begotten in that manner. Yet a victim must be human in kind in order to be considered a *voluntary* victim.

It may be asked why such a physically, morally, and spiritually pure human victim cannot be the product of a human sexual union. For the answer, it is necessary to bring up the murky story of the origin of sexual unions, as told in the Bible and in Tanakh. In the etiological story of the Fall, there had been no sexual union before the Fall. It was only after the Fall that God himself decreed sexual unions. He did so in order to ensure the continuation of the human race beyond Adam and Eve, who had now become liable to die, when they chose to eat of the fruit of the Tree of the Knowledge of Good and Evil. It was at that point that God decreed that "the woman's desire shall be for her husband" (Genesis 3:16 NRSV), thereby providing a means of evading the abortion of the human race, and of continuing it beyond the assured death of Adam and Eve. In fact, it was only at Genesis 4:1 that Adam finally consummated the union, and the two went on to produce Cain and Abel. Given this murky history of the origin of sexual unions, how would a child begotten in such a manner be the Son of God?

Now, everyone born human must have a human mother. If, however, an intended sacrificial human victim were to have had a human father as well, it is clear from the quoted scripture passages, including Jesus's own remark, that he certainly would not be without sin. Hence, the *father* of the intended sacrificial victim cannot be human, once given that he has a human mother; otherwise, he would not be spotless in the required human manner.

It would appear, therefore, that Jesus, the intended expiating victim, would require a virgin mother, but not a human father. Joseph himself was assured of this in the vision that God granted him to allay his misgivings over the looming parthenogenesis of his son. One notes, in consequence of this, that it would only be through his mother that Jesus, the intended expiating victim, could have been related to David and to Abraham, and not through Joseph, Mary's betrothed. Jesus himself appears to have denied patrilineal descent from David when he quoted the Psalm in which David acknowledges Jesus as Lord (Matthew 22:31–35, Mark 12:35–37).

So far, it does seem that Jesus's spotlessness requires the absence of a male human parent. How, though, can this spotlessness be assured, given that he does have a human mother? It would appear that there is a twofold way to do so: first, by Jesus becoming incarnate of a mother who is virgin, thus completely eliminating the need for a human sire (the blessedness among women); second, by the immaculate or sinless conception of Jesus's own mother, augmented by a fullness of grace, which would guarantee his mother's own continuous insulation from sin. Both requirements were acknowledged at the annunciation by the archangel Gabriel when he saluted Mary as blessed among women and full of grace.

Lest the second be thought redundant, it only need be mentioned that the Holy Spirit would not be likely to incarnate Jesus out of a sin-bearing mother's body, even if that mother was herself immaculately conceived; in other words, in a human body that was not from its own conception *forward* freed of all sin. Accordingly, the mother of Jesus required not only initial, but also enduring sinlessness. This would mean that in her own origin, she would be immaculately conceived, and, by virtue of a fullness of grace, she would remain spotless through Jesus's own birth. As to the rest, would there have been a Judaic male who, once assured in a numinous vision that his betrothed's child was conceived by the power of the Most High, would subsequently pursue relations with her? Would there have been a Judaic woman who, told by an archangel she was to be the mother of the Son of the Most High, would countenance such a pursuit?

And yet, if Jesus Christ had to be born of an immaculately conceived virgin mother in order to secure his own spotlessness, his lack of a human paternal ancestry would completely prevent him from being a male descendant through Aaron's line. Accordingly, he could not be a priest in the order of Aaron. It appears, however, that descent from Aaron was not in every case a precondition for being a priest of God, as we saw in the case of Moses.

As to Jesus, it was just as well that he was not descended from Aaron. The obligation under protocol of every Aaronic high priest to first offer a sacrifice for his own sins before he could offer an oblation for the sins of the people could not have been observed by Jesus, since he himself remained without sin. That obligation would have been rendered meaningless in his case, since he would not have had any sins of his own that would require an initial cleansing sacrifice. Besides, in seeking forgiveness for the sins of the people, the high priest was obliged, again by protocol, to intercede with God. Here, too, no such obligation could pertain to Jesus, since he himself was well able to forgive others' sins on his own authority and directly, and did so with no need to intercede with his Father (Matthew 9:2, 5; Mark 2:5, 9; Luke 5:20, 5:23, 7:48). In Jesus's case, the only thing that would require the Father's intervention would be the expiation of sin, and that he was scheduled to bring about all at once, and once and for all, on the hill of Golgotha.

Herein lies the crucial difference between the priestly function of Jesus and that of the Aaronic priests: while they only really interceded for the *forgiveness* of sins, not righteousness through atonement, Jesus had come to *expiate* sin, atone for sin, and also offer everlasting life. After all, if the animal sacrifices were effective atonement, what need would there be in Judah for Jesus to come and die and atone for sins? Assuredly, the same divine dispensations and personal accomplishment that secured the sinlessness of Jesus as a prospective officiating high priest have also secured his spotlessness as a prospective sacrificial victim.

Jesus was to be the victim without sin, except that, in his case, he would be so by observing the full spirit of the law, and, whenever necessary, its letter as well. As Jesus himself said, he had come to fulfill the law. It was not as if Jesus did not encounter opportunities for sin. He was subject to the law and was keenly tested under it. Right after his encounter with John at the Jordan River, he proceeded into the wilderness to be tempted by Satan. At this prelude to his mission, for forty days he had to resist all Satanic blandishments and succeed in remaining free from any sin of commission or omission. According to Hebrews 4:15, Jesus was liable to the same infirmities as we are, tested in all points, but without sinning. He was tested by the people, tested by Peter, and most severely tempted toward the conclusion of his mission while in the garden of Gethsemane. In spite of the worldly joys set before him by Satanic blandishments and the rabbinical privileges he could have enjoyed, he chose to proceed to the cross and die an ignominous death.

As to the sin-redeeming sacrifice of Jesus itself, it could not be conducted except by a priest; in fact, it called for a priest who was himself without sin. Since no one could really be made sinless by the prior slaughter of an animal, Jesus, who was the only first male child of an immaculately conceived mother, and who never incurred any sin of his own, thus became the only one who could be that priest. It is thus that it fell on Jesus to be both victim and high priest at his own self-sacrifice for the sins of the whole world.

Still, even if descent from Aaron was not quite necessary for a priestly designation, every would-be priest must be correctly recognized or acknowledged to be such in order to offer sacrifices for others before God. It is surely for this reason that scripture carefully clarifies that Jesus was indeed a priest, whose priesthood was, however, not in the order of Aaron, but in that of Melchizedek, a priest of God Most High. Given the supposed meaning of *Melchizedek* (Righteousness is my King), could it be that that very designation speaks to righteousness, and so sinlessness, in a priest of this order? At Jeremiah 23:6 (NRSV), we read: "In his days, Judah will be saved, and Israel will live in safety, and this is the name by which he will be called 'The Lord is our righteousness.' In an address that applies to Jesus, Psalm 45:6–7 (NRSV) says, "Your throne, O God, endures forever and ever. Your royal scepter is a scepter of equity; you love righteousness and hate wickedness."

The highest priestly function was to offer the sacrifices of the people to God. A sacrifice could be offered for a variety of reasons, such as giving thanks, for purification from ceremonial blemish, or for favors sought or received. At its heart, though, sacrifice was a sin-offering made only by the high priest, first for his own sins and then for the sins of the people—typically a bull for the priest and a ram for the people.

To start with, the sacrificial animals, which were themselves held to be antecedently without sin or blemish, were saddled with the sins of the priest and those of the people respectively. In this way, the obligation of paying the wages of sin by death was putatively transferred to the animals, whose lives immediately became forfeit. That relocation of sins preceded, and was distinct from, their intended atonement through the death of the victim. Since life was understood to be in the blood (Leviticus 17:11, Deuteronomy 12:23), the exacted satisfaction involved the shedding of blood. Hence, it was only with the shedding of the blood of those animals that sins were thought to have been expiated. It was as if the sacrificial animals died in place of the priest and the people, and, in a sense, they did.

Evidently, there was much in all of this that was pro forma. It was, of course, only in a supposititious way that the bulls and goats could be deemed to have been without sin themselves, and so able to take on the sins of others. In fact, they were sinless purely by their not having ever infringed prescribed law, since they were in no way subject to any such law. As Paul was to observe, without law there would be no sin.

In this, however, the temple sacrifices did foreshadow the sacrifice of Jesus. If those sacrifices had been effective atonement, there would hardly have been any need in Judah for Jesus to come and die to atone for sins.

The fact that Jesus incurred no personal sin does pose a problem for the almost universally held belief that he received a baptism from John the Baptist. It is true that those who saw Jesus immersed in the Jordan without hearing the exchange between him and John would naturally have thought that he was receiving a baptism. How, though, could this be, when John's baptism was a baptism of *repentance*, whereas Jesus by universal consent had no sin to repent? Jesus presumably knew that he himself was without sin, but did John?

In all the Synoptic Gospels, it is assumed that, when Jesus approached John at the Jordan River, it was to seek baptism. At Matthew 3:14, even the Baptist evidently believed this. Nevertheless, he demurred, saying that it was he who should be seeking baptism of Jesus. It is not enough to say that the Baptist thought he was being confronted by his superior, whom he should accordingly not be baptizing. Since John's baptism was a baptism of repentance only, superiority alone should not disqualify a would-be recipient, but only his utter lack of sin. A sin-possessing superior would still be subject to baptism.

Since the Baptist claims that he had no previous knowledge of Jesus (John 1:33) when Jesus came to him, the only possible reason for his reluctance must have been an instinctive realization that Jesus was without sin, and could not receive a baptism specifically designed for those with sins to repent. Of course, Jesus, too, knew that he himself was without sin, and so had no use for a baptism of repentance. So, if Jesus did not come to the Baptist to receive baptism, why did he?

The answer lies in Jesus's rejoinder to the Baptist after he declined to baptize him. Jesus had declared that it was fitting to observe all righteousness (Matthew 3:15). The Greek word used is *dikaiosyne*, which was, of course, the gospel writer's attempt to render the Hebrew *tzedakah* into Greek. While *dikaiosyne* does mean righteousness, *tzedakah* actually means obedience to the will of God. So a *tzaddik*, or righteous person, is one who obeys God's will or command. The key is obedience, which of course does imply a prior demand. In consequence, what Jesus said to the Baptist meant that it was needful or fitting to obey God's will or demand. This insight about what Jesus meant comes from *The*

Jewish Annotated Bible, edited by Amy-Jill Levine and Marc Zvi Brettler, Oxford University Press.

What demand or command of God could Jesus have had in mind? To be sure, there existed no command requiring baptism of anyone, baptism being completely voluntary, resting as it did on one's own inclination and feeling of guilt, which Jesus did not have. In placing a constraint on the Baptist, Jesus must have been thinking of something quite other than a baptism, something actually demanded by some law, and whatever command Jesus was invoking would be clarified in the account given by the Baptist in the pericope, John 1:29–34 (NRSV).

In that pericope, John the Baptist was reminiscing in his own voice on this first encounter with Jesus, an encounter that had convinced him that Jesus was the Lamb of God, who would atone for the sins of the world, and whose consequently implied spotlessness would mean that he was personally without sin or other blemish. Encouraged by Jesus at this juncture to fulfill righteousness or obey God's will, the Baptist relented and immersed Jesus. Thereupon, two things happened: there was a declarative voice from heaven, and a descending dove that landed and perched on Jesus. In his reminiscence, the Baptist testified (verses 32–33): "I saw the Spirit descending from heaven like a dove, and it remained on him. I myself did not know him, but the one who sent me to baptize with water said to me: 'he, upon whom you see the Spirit descend and remain, is the one who baptizes with the Holy Spirit.'" In other gospels, it is reported that the declarative voice from heaven said that Jesus was the beloved Son of God (Matthew 3:17, Mark 1:11, Luke 3:22). In the present pericope, the Baptist was able to say authoritatively (verse 34), "And I myself have testified that this is the Son of God," presumably saying this because he himself had heard what the declaration from heaven said. If a baptism of repentance, and not

Jesus's own insistence that he be immersed, had been connected with the voice from heaven or the descent of the dove, would not the Baptist, who was reminiscing in his own voice, have recalled that connection at this point?

Why and to whom had the Baptist testified that Jesus was the Son of God? John the Baptist had said (John 1:31) that the reason he himself had come baptizing with water was so that he could reveal Jesus to Israel—reveal him, according to his testimony, as the Lamb of God, who would be atoning for sins, and as the beloved Son of God. Even though there was no law mandating the reception of baptism, there was a law requiring two or three witnesses against or in support of anyone facing a capital charge. Deuteronomy 17:6 (NRSV) records: "On the evidence of two or three witnesses the death sentence shall be executed; a person must not be put to death on the evidence of only one witness," while 19:15 states, "A single witness shall not suffice to convict a person of any crime or wrongdoing in connection with any offense that may be committed. Only on the evidence of two or three witnesses shall a charge be sustained." Indeed, Matthew 18:16 (NRSV) similarly reads: "But if you are not listened to, take one or two others along with you, so that every word may be confirmed by the evidence of two or three witnesses."

While Jesus was probably not already involved with an allegation of "sin or wickedness" when he visited the Baptist, he certainly subsequently became so involved. For example, at John 5:18, he was challenged to justify his repeated claim to being the Son of God, thereby making himself of a kind with God. Jesus had just healed a paralytic man on a Sabbath. In response to strong objections, he claimed (5:17): "My Father is still working until now, and I also am working." This response made his interlocutors wish all the more to kill him, "because he was not only breaking the Sabbath, but was also calling God his own Father, thereby making himself equal to God." To counter this accusation of the capital sin of blasphemy, Jesus needed to advance at least one or two additional witnesses to back him up in compliance with the law that he had urged the Baptist to join him in obeying. It was to this end that the encounter with the Baptist was of immense help, as is clear from Jesus's further remarks.

Jesus reminded his present accusers of the priests and Levites who had been sent earlier as emissaries to John the Baptist to ask him whether he, the Baptist himself, was the awaited Messiah (1:19–23). The Baptist truthfully denied that he was, but added that they already had an as yet unrecognized person present among them, the latchet of whose sandals he himself was unworthy to unfasten.

Adding to this, Jesus pointed to the dazzling works that his Father had given him to complete, which should have convinced them (5:36) that he himself was the Messiah. His opponents, though, had been inclined to dismiss those miracles as evidence of the workings of the Devil. Nor would they accept the testimony of scripture (5:39), in which Moses and the prophets had spoken beforehand of him. It was the refusal to accept Jesus's word or those testimonies that now compelled Jesus to resort to two others, the personal testimony of the Father on his behalf (the voice from heaven) and the word of the Baptist (5:33, 37; vide 1:33–34).

The testimony of the highly esteemed Baptist, that Jesus was the Son of God, should really have freed Jesus from the accusation; for, as the Son of God, Jesus would share a nature with his father, God, and thus be divine, just as any son would share a nature with his human father and be human. Besides, as the son of Mary, Jesus would also be human. Hence, in being at one and the same time the Son of God and the son of Mary, Jesus was at one and the same time both divine and human, both God and man.

It is perhaps interesting that with their inquiries about Jesus, the Pharisees, priests, and Levites were actually now in possession of the concepts required for the intuition of the Trinity. John, whom they generally held in awe, had corroborated Jesus's claim to being the Son of the Father, and so, as they themselves feared, of a divine nature, and thus the second person in the Godhead. As to the third person, would the Spirit of God, the Ruach Elohim (Genesis 1:2) or the Ruach haKodesh whom the Sanhedrin acknowledged, be other than divine in nature?

It would be a mistake to treat the last as an abstract idea. A comparison between Spirit locutions in Tanakh and Spirit locutions in the New Testament is eye-opening. In the former, there are locutions such as the following: from Genesis 1:2 (TNIV): "The Spirit of God was hovering over the waters"; Genesis 41:38: "One in whom is the Spirit of God?" Numbers 24:2: "the Spirit of God came on him"; Job 33:4: "The Spirit of God has made me"; Ezekiel 11:24: "The Spirit lifted me up and brought me to the exiles in Babylonia in the vision given by the Spirit of God"; Matthew 3:16 (NRSV): "And he saw the Spirit of God descending like a dove"; Matthew 4:1 (NRSV): "Then Jesus was led by the Spirit into the wilderness to be tempted"; Matthew 12:18 (NRSV): "I will put my Spirit upon him"; Matthew 12:28 (NRSV): "But if it is by the Spirit of God that I drive out demons"; Acts 8:39 (NRSV): "The Spirit of the Lord caught Philip away and the eunuch saw him no more"; Romans 8:9: "If indeed the Spirit of God lives in you"; Romans 8:14: "For those who are led by the Spirit of God are the children of God"; 1 Corinthians 3:16: "Don't you know that you yourselves are God's temple and that God's Spirit dwells in your midst?"; 1 Peter 4:14: "For the Spirit of glory and of God rests on you."

Now, as to that sinlessness of Jesus, implied in his being the atoning Lamb of God, he did not simply find himself always without sin. Born without sin, he actively maintained his sinless state. Thus, during his encounter with the Devil in the wilderness for forty days, he showed himself stalwart in withstanding the Devil's wiles. A second Adam, Jesus was obliged to show this stalwartness if he was to proceed to the task of redeeming the world. He was obliged to persevere in his own sinless state throughout his life. Only in this way, as a victim consciously and deliberately without sin, could Jesus's sacrifice be truly efficacious. As for those temple sacrificial animals, they were simply captives upon which pro forma attempts were made to foist human sins. They were forcibly robbed of their own lives with absolutely no moral exchange involved. Involuntary victimhood points out the way but is without salvific efficacy. Its real hope is for forgiveness, not the righteousness that alone saves. As Hebrews 10:4 puts it: "it is impossible for the blood of bulls and goats to take away sins." Hence, even after the countless animals sacrificed by the high priests, there would still be not one righteous.

As to expiation, such sacrifice would only be for atonement, not salvation or the securing of endless life. Without expiation, however, there would be no salvation, only endless death. Accordingly, since the Sadducees could not see any avenues from forgiveness to salvation, or the securing of everlasting life after death, they tended to see religion only as ethical and not at all as salvific.

For sacrifice to be really expiatory, though, both the assumption of sin and the surrender of life must be completely voluntary on the victim's part. It is surely for this reason that Jesus said of his own life in the good shepherd discourse at John 10:18 (NRSV): "No one takes it from me, but I lay it down of my own accord." In keeping with this, Jesus was not captured in the garden of Gethsemane, but simply surrendered himself, after first exacting immunity from arrest for his disciples.

At no time was Jesus a merely passive victim. He was always a self-motivated and self-directed agent, step by step enacting the definite plan, which was foreordained and foreknown by God (Acts 2:23), a plan that was to culminate in human salvation and the promise of everlasting life. Jesus's final journey to Jerusalem, his institution of the Mass at the Last Supper, his arrest at Gethsemane, condemnation and capital sentence, torture and crucifixion were all well-laid-out components of this earthly campaign. Never was he an involuntary victim of either the players or the circumstances in this cosmic drama. The reason is that Jesus came to fulfill prophecy, not to confirm it. A prophecy is not a prediction. When a prediction comes to pass, it is not fulfilled, but confirmed, in attestation of its accuracy. A prophecy, on the other hand, cannot simply come to pass but is, by reason of the element of intentionality embedded in it, fulfilled. Accordingly, a prophecy does not simply turn out to be true, but is, like a promise, carried out and fulfilled. Jesus was the fulfiller of prophecy, not its verifier.

With the genius of hindsight, it is easy for us to see that centuries of prophecy, commencing with Moses, would not have had for their focus the mere toppling of the distantly future Roman rule. The conquering Christ came into the world to confront and vanquish a foe that was invincible to all earthly power; namely, the everlasting death let loose on us by our willfulness. In accomplishing this feat, Jesus was to carry out three distinct but interrelated actions.

CHAPTER 3

THE THREE SALVIFIC ACTIONS OF JESUS CHRIST

Jesus's first action consisted in his sacrificial assumption of our sins; his second action consisted in his paying through his own death "the wages of sin," a debt that he acquired from us, and his third action consisted in actually overcoming death through his own resurrection. With those actions, he severed the link between sin and everlasting death. Surely, it is those three actions: voluntary assumption of sins, consequent death, and triumphant resurrection, which are envisaged at Romans 4:25. Jesus died for our trespasses (which he had taken over), and, by the victory of his resurrection, he gave us the guarantee of everlasting life. This is why Jesus could declare himself to be the resurrection and, thereby, the life.

Jesus came into the world not to forgive our sins or simply to take them away (for, after all, sin can be forgiven from heaven), but rather to establish something greater, which could be accomplished nowhere except on earth; namely, to forge for us a sure path to eternal life, thus restoring what was forfeited with the onset of sin. Several passages in the Bible indicate that much, most famously John 3:16 (NRSV): "For God so loved the world that he gave his only Son, so that everyone who trusts in him may have eternal life, and not be utterly destroyed"; and, from the mouth of Jesus himself, "I came that they may have life, and have it abundantly" (John 10:10 NRSV).

It is just this understanding that Jesus came to secure a path to everlasting life for us, and not simply to relieve us of our sins, that drove Paul to exclaim that those who placed their faith in Jesus Christ and set their hopes on him would, of all people, be most to be pitied in the event that Jesus Christ had not been able to shatter the bonds of death and come back to life. For, in such a case, while he would still have assumed our sins, and even expiated them through his own death, he would not have done enough to show that a person who is once laden with sin can nevertheless evade everlasting death.

Actually, since Jesus would all the same have died in our place, then, if that were to have been his entire aim, there should be no cause whatever why we should be pitied, for no subsequent resurrection or absence of it could in any way affect the fact of the vicarious death itself. It therefore remains that the only reason why those who trust in Christ would be most to be pitied would be if Christ's true purpose were not simply the remission of our sins, or even their expiation through his dying, but rather the forging of a path to eternal life for us by his breaking the link between sin and eternal death. Had he remained in the shackles of death, failing to secure eternal life for himself after he became laden with our sins and died for them, how could he have possibly verified for others and bestowed on them what he would have been unable to achieve for himself?

With Jesus's resurrection, it thus becomes entirely appropriate that Paul should declare at Romans 6:23 that it is eternal life in Christ Jesus our Lord that is the gift of God! John likewise alerts: "I write these things to you who believe in the name of the Son of God, so that you may know that you have eternal life" (1 John 5:13

NRSV). In this, the remission of sins is an indispensable turning point, but by no means the pivotal one.

For the rest, what is required is to explicate those three actions of Jesus Christ, and to determine the distinct point at which he can be said to have performed each of them.

Chapter 4

Certain Aspects of a Sacrificial Victim and an Officiant

There are compelling reasons to believe that it was during the Last Supper, and well before the crucifixion, that Jesus sacrificially assumed our sins and, in so doing, rendered himself liable to pay their price, a price whose final installment he paid when he allowed himself to be slain.

In his self-sacrifice for the sins of the whole world, Jesus was obliged to be his own officiating priest, since there was nobody else who could have officiated, offering Jesus as the victim, without first needing to offer a separate sacrifice for his own sins—an ineffectual gesture since the profferer of the preliminary sacrifice would still be a sinner in the eyes of God. The same reason that precluded Jesus from receiving a baptism of repentance worked again in this priestly function. Alone without sin, and hence not standing in need of a prior cleansing sacrifice for himself, Jesus was uniquely fitted to officiate at that particular sacrifice by which our sins were assumed.

The animals accepted in temple sacrifices were first examined by the priests, and the seal of approval duly placed on them only if they were found to be without spot or other animal blemish. For the same reason, Jesus too had to pass scrutiny as a victim in this sacrifice of the assumption of our sins: he was viewed, and he was declared by the Father, God, to be well-pleasing, having been found to be without physical or other human blemish. In accordance with this, John the Baptist was inspired to pronounce him the Lamb of God who takes away the sins of the world (John 1:29). Jesus himself signified as much, when he urged, "Do not work for the food that perishes, but for the food that endures for eternal life, which the Son of Man will give you; for it is on him that God the Father has set his seal" (John 6:27 NRSV), and, by Judaic tradition, when the sacrificial victim is not incinerated, it is consumed—as food—by those for whom it was sacrificed.

In all certainty, Jesus would be required, at the very point of being presented as victim at this sacrifice of the assumption of our sins, to have remained without blemish, continuing to be up to the certification of the Father, God, or he would not at that juncture be an acceptable sacrificial victim. This point is clearly of decisive importance in fixing the three salvific actions of Jesus.

From all accounts, Jesus did not have the physical appearance of an acceptable victim at the time of his actual crucifixion. He had been buffeted, spat upon, inhumanly scourged and grotesquely lacerated, his body a platform of physical insults. The description of the suffering servant in Isaiah 53 offers a template for Jesus's outward appearance on the verge of his crucifixion. In such a badly compromised condition, he could not possibly be perceived as an unspotted, unblemished, and acceptable sacrificial victim, and so could not have been advanced at this juncture as a victim for sacrifice. Consequently, that self-sacrifice whereby he took over our own sins and acquired responsibility for them could not have been only then occurring at the crucifixion, but must have taken place earlier at a time when he was still morally, physically, and ritually unimpaired.

It should also be mentioned that, if Jesus himself is the officiant, then, at the point of sacrifice, he would need to be without ritual, moral, or spiritual blemish, otherwise he would like every other high priest (except Melchizedek) first need a sanctifying sacrifice on his own behalf. This, after all, was the point of the priest's sacrifice for himself before performing a cleansing sacrifice on behalf of the people. In any case, Jesus's same bloodied condition on the brink of his crucifixion, which would have prevented him from being an acceptable sacrificial victim for atonement, would also have ritually disqualified him at that point from being officiant or priest at any sacrifice, let alone at the sacrifice of the Lamb of God. In more senses than one, the victim must be clean, and the officiating priest must come with clean hands.

By the time of the crucifixion, however, Jesus, who earlier on would have been the only human being fit to be High Priest at the sacrifice of the Lamb of God by reason of his physical integrity and moral and spiritual purity, would now no longer be ritually fit to be presented de novo either as the Lamb of God or as God's officiating high priest. It would appear to follow that that was not the occasion when Jesus initially sacrificed himself to be bearer of our sins, let alone acted as the sacrificing high priest.

A selected sacrificial victim in an atonement sacrifice was first saddled with the sins to be expiated before being, in consequence of those sins, condemned to death and slain. That sequence was essential for sins to be thought to have been atoned for. At the time that Jesus was nominated for victimization by Caiaphas, after he learned of the raising of Lazarus, Jesus was wholly unblemished and from that perspective carried, still uncompromised, the seal of the Father, God (John 11:50–53). And yet, at the time when the assembled Sanhedrin ratified its capital sentence on Jesus, he would have had to be already saddled with our sins, or that condemnation to death would not have been prospectively expiatory of those sins.

Where, then, and when, did Jesus take over the sins of the world?

CHAPTER 5

WHERE AND WHEN JESUS CHRIST TOOK OVER OUR SINS

A good possibility would be the night of the Last Supper, when Jesus instituted the eucharistic Mass. It was then that he spoke those words by which he seemed to assume sins: "This is my body which is on your behalf." Those words rendered him directly accountable for our sins. Only Jesus was without prior sin; hence only Jesus, and not the high priest Caiaphas, could have accomplished that sacrificial transfer of sins. Now heavily laden with those sins, Jesus was in fact to see his fortunes so rapidly glissade that some of his compatriots would be quick to see his woes as a plain and unambiguous proof of God's disfavor (cf Isaiah 53:4). Those consequences racked him with scant delay, commencing with the lugubrious episode in the garden of Gethsemane and ending with the tragedy on the hill of Golgotha.

Although Jesus always had the power to merely forgive our sins and not actually assume them, he could not simply extirpate them, as was made plain in Gethsemane. That aspect of his self-sacrifice, which took place in the course of the Last Supper, was wholly for the remission of our sins to us through his taking ownership of them, in full knowledge that the necessary atonement for those as yet unexpurgated sins would cost him dearly. In this sin-laden condition, Jesus would need another high priest to manage his slaying. He certainly could not commit suicide. That other high priest would be Caiaphas. But, both on account of the proscription against human sacrifice for all who live under Judaic Law and because of the futility of trying to purify himself by a prior cleansing sacrifice, Caiaphas would indeed require a *Gentile* agency that would be free of all such constraints. That blood-shedding expiation would follow later, and only after the run through the agony of Gethsemane, the inquisition of the Sanhedrin, the flagellation by the Romans, and the trudging along Jesus's via dolorosa to the hill of Golgotha.

This is probably the occasion to recall that sacrifice does not inherently require death or the shedding of blood. Grain sacrifice is bloodless, and so are libations. When the Israelites made to God a sacrifice of the first male child that opened the womb, this meant no more than their ceding the firstborn son to the service of God, and when the sons of Levi were themselves sacrificed in a wave offering in lieu of the first sons of all Israelite women, their blood was not shed (Numbers 8:15). Mothers do nothing bloody when they sacrifice themselves for their children. Nor do unremunerated caregivers do anything bloody when they sacrifice themselves for their charge. Conspicuously, ordained priests as well as brothers and sisters in religious orders, who embrace celibacy and consecrate their entire lives to the service of God and humanity, generally do not shed their blood. Indeed, Jesus's own self-sacrifice at the Mass of the Last Supper did not draw any blood. Actually, that fact would seem to be the real reason why the church can carry out his command and "do this" in a similarly bloodless manner, and also the true reason why the sacrifice of the Mass can, without euphemism or understatement, be always labeled "bloodless." Only a *living* being can assume the sins of another, just as only a *dying* being can expiate the sins of another. Always, the assumption of sins is bloodless; their atonement is not (Hebrews 9:22).

One important reason why the matter is not usually presented quite this way is reflected in the different emphasis of the eucharistic prayers in the order of Mass. These prayers deliberately use words of institution that are at some variance from the received Greek texts in order to highlight the atonement of sins and submerge their mere forgiveness in their expiation. Those prayers systematically employ the future tense where the Greek texts invariably use the present tense. Those prayers say, "Take this, all of you, and eat it: this is my body which will be given up for you." Of the blood, they say, "Take this, all of you, and drink from it. This is the chalice of my blood, the blood of the new and everlasting covenant. It will be shed for you and for all that sins may be forgiven." This preference for the future tense accurately fits in with the vicarious atonement, which clearly assumes a preceding remission through the assumption of sins by Jesus. That assumption of sins actually occurred on the night of the Last Supper, while their expiation or atonement was only to occur many hours later on the cross.

As to the Greek texts themselves, they say the following:

a. 1 Corinthians 11:24–25: "And, after giving thanks, he broke it, and said: This is my body which is on your behalf < in your place?> (ὑπὲρ, *hyper*): this do in recall (re-call?) of me.

   "And in the same manner, the after-dinner cup, saying: this cup is the new covenant in my blood. This do as often as you drink it in recall (re-call?) of me."

b. Mark 14:22–24. "And, while they were still eating, he took a loaf of wheat bread, and after blessing it, he broke it and gave it to them, and said: Take; this is my body.

"Then, he took a cup, and when he had given thanks, he gave it to them, (and said): Drink of it, all of you.

"And he said to them: This is the blood of my covenant which is being poured out (ἐκχυννόμενον *ekchynnomenon*) for the sake of many."

c. Matthew 26:26–28: "While they were still eating, Jesus took a loaf of bread, and after blessing it, he broke it, and as he was giving it to the disciples he said: Take, eat, this is my body;

"then he took a cup, gave thanks, and gave it to them, saying: Drink of it, all of you,

"for this is my blood of the covenant which is being poured out for many for the removal of sins" (ἐκχυννόμενον, *ekchynnomenon*).

d. Luke 22:19–20: "Then he took a loaf of bread, and when he had given thanks, he broke it, and gave it to them, saying: This is my body which is being given up (διδόμενον, *didomenon*) on your account. This do in recall of me.

"And he did the same with the cup after dinner, saying: This cup is the new covenant in my blood which is being poured out (ἐκχυννόμενον, *ekchynnomenon*) on your account."

Of these sources, Luke and 1 Corinthians place "the body" in context. It is "hyper hymon"; in other words, "on your behalf," "for your sakes," or "on your account," or, best of all, "in your place." Bloodlessly, he had now given himself for us for the removal of our sins from us, though not yet for their expiation. In Luke, the use of the present participle, διδόμενον, *didomenon*, as does the use of the present participle ἐκχυννόμενον, *ekchynnomenon* in all three Synoptic Gospels, indicates that this particular sacrifice is occurring pari passu with the speaking of the words, and is not shelved till some future time. Does it not seem that the time to seal the covenant relating to Jesus's assignation of his body for our sins is the very time of the assignation itself, especially since the apostles in attendance must enter into the covenant before they have a chance to disperse as they were soon afterwards to do?

With Jesus's words the bread there and then became his flesh in the required manner (to be discussed in the following chapter), and the wine there and then became his blood, and in pronouncing his body as being for us, he effectively assumed our sins. He had now clearly sacrificed himself for us.

Even though Jesus "through the eternal Spirit offered himself without blemish to God" (Hebrews 9:14 NRSV) in order to save humanity from our transgressions, the last time that he could be said to have been without spot or blemish would have been at the Last Supper, prior to the utterance of the words of institution by which he became encumbered with our sins. He very probably could not be described as being without blemish at any point between his departure from the site of the Last Supper to enter the garden of Gethsemane and his crucifixion on the hill of Golgotha. At that Last Supper, he was both high priest and sacrificial victim. It was thus there that he initiated the all-embracing action that would stretch to the crucifixion.

Now laden with our sins, his forlorn situation became evident from the moment he entered the garden of Gethsemane. Gethsemane was where the punishment for the sins of the whole world, which he was then carrying, began to be exacted from Jesus.

For it was there that Jesus first revealed existential experience of humankind's burden of sin, and became so distressed that he began feeling like death (Matthew 26:38). It was there that, in his despondent condition, blood seeped into his sweat (Luke 24:44) in a condition medically known as hematidrosis, which is usually spurred on by intense anxiety and the fear of approaching death. It was in the garden of Gethsemane that Jesus experienced dread and foreboding and alienation of the sort induced by one's own consciousness of profound sin. So crushing was this consciousness that, in dismay, Jesus flung himself on the ground, "offering up with loud cries and tears both prayers and supplications to the One who was able to save him from death" (Hebrews 2:17–18 NRSV).

Three times Jesus entreated his Father to relieve him of the cup and save him from death: "My Father, if it is possible, let this cup pass from me; yet, not what I want, but what you want" (Matthew 26:34 NRSV). Three times his Father declined that particular request. The reason was that, once the Father had laid upon him at his own request the iniquity of the whole world (Isaiah 53:6, John 1:29, 1 John 2:2), Jesus could not deliver eternal life to us without first expiating those sins through his own death, followed by a resurrection. Those steps were ineluctable. Still, even though it was not possible to let that particular cup pass, and Jesus had to resign himself to that fact by submerging his own will to the Father's will, the Father heard him on account of his piety (Hebrews 2:16), and granted him the strength and composure to bear his ordeal with long-suffering dignity. From that point on to the most bitter conclusion, Jesus's comportment was manifestly calm and stoical.

The cup in question was the cup of God's wrath (sometimes said to be a bowl), and is well-known in Hebrew lore. God said to Jeremiah (25:15f NRSV): "Take from my hand this cup of the wine of wrath, and make all the nations to whom I send you drink it." Ezekiel (23:31–34) depicted it as a cup of horror and destruction that brought scorn and derision among other miseries upon those who drank it. Habakkuk (2:16) reported that it was destructive of glory, while Job (21:20) prayed that his detractors might drink of the wrath of the Almighty and see their destruction with their own eyes. At Mark 10:39, Jesus told the two presumptuous sons of Zebedee that they would indeed drink of the cup that was in store for him. At Psalm 75, verse 8, God pours out the cup of wine down to the dregs, and all the wicked must drain it. This is the cup that Jesus undertook to drain on behalf of all mankind.

That cup would last Jesus from Gethsemane to Golgotha. It would stay on his lips during the encounter with the Sanhedrin. God's wrath would beleaguer him in the outrageous abuse by the temple guards and in the truculent flagellation by Roman legionnaires. Still God's wrath would not be assuaged. There would be the greatest woe of all, the actual payment of the wages of sin. That step in particular could not be evaded, as Jesus in the garden of Gethsemane had hoped it would be. It is little wonder that, coming at the tail end of an excruciating night and day, that last step caused Jesus to feel as if he had been abandoned by his Father: "My God, my God, why have you abandoned me?" he moaned. As a matter of fact, the whole of Psalm 22, which Jesus was then bringing to life, perfectly fit his ongoing plight and impending deliverance.

The question, though, is why God would inflict this cup of venomous wrath on Jesus, a man who had not personally offended him in any way. The case of Job sheds absolutely no light here. While it is true that Job suffered gratuitously, and not in consequence of any offense to God, he was really under demonic assault and not God's wrath, for the sole purpose of revealing to Satan Job's unshakeable fidelity to God, and the capacity of a human being for unconditional, nontransactional love of the sort preached by Jesus (Matthew 5:44, 22:37; Mark 12:30; Luke 6:27, 35, 10:27; John 13:34, 15:12) and explicated by Paul (1 Corinthians 13:4–13). It was Job, the steadfast, who said, "Even though he slay me, yet will I trust in him" (Job 13:15, alternate reading of the Hebrew text). In the minor example of the blinded Tobias, God permitted his trial to give an example of patience to posterity, as of "holy Job" (Tobit 2:12).

In the case of Jesus of Nazareth, demons themselves appealed to his generosity when they encountered him, and implored him for lenient treatment. It is inconceivable that Satan and his demons would have had the temerity to launch on Jesus, as they did on Job, an assault that would have been bound to fail. God did not pour his wrath on Job or on Tobias; God did pour his wrath on Jesus of Nazareth as the bearer of all our sins. God's display of wrath is never gratuitous, being always a response to sin.

Again, what could have provoked the tremendous torrent of wrath that swept Jesus from the agony of Gethsemane to the crucifixion at Golgotha? It could only have been the collocation of the sins of the whole world in the person of the man, Jesus of Nazareth. Without a doubt, in the garden of Gethsemane, Jesus of Nazareth was already burdened with our sins, and, without a doubt, he could only have acquired them during his self-sacrifice at the Mass of the Last Supper, for when he began that Mass, he was still ritually pure and without sin, and so did not need a preliminary cleansing sacrifice for himself! However, with the words of institution relating to his body as stated in the Greek texts, he took over the sins of the whole world. That feat of love showed the mercy of God toward us. The coming expiation on the cross of Golgotha would fulfill the justice of God and satisfy his holiness.

Chapter 6

The Nature of the Real Presence

By tradition, the flesh of a sacrificed victim was made available for consumption by the beneficiaries of the sacrifice, unless it was a thoroughly incinerated holocaust. In the case of an atonement sacrifice, the flesh was typically made available to the high priest and his family, except when it was an atonement for the high priest himself, in which case the holocaust was completely incinerated. At the time of the Last Supper when Jesus was both high priest and became the lamb that bore the sins of the world, the victim's flesh was his, and, since he was High Priest, the victim's flesh, his own flesh, became available for consumption by his family. Now his assembled apostles had by that time become his brethren by adoption (Matthew 28:10, Mark 3:34, Luke 14:12, John 7:10), and so had become eligible to eat the flesh of the victim, in the present case Jesus's own flesh. By law and tradition, it is thus only by becoming Jesus's brethren that we too can so partake. However, since all those who hear the word of God and do it providentially become Jesus's brethren (Luke 6:21), we can in this way all become Jesus's brethren, and thereby acquire the right to partake of his body.

"Take, eat, this is my body," Jesus said (Matthew 26:26 NRSV). But what of his blood, the blood of the sacrificial victim, given that there existed no tradition of drinking blood, or, for that matter, of eating human flesh? Jesus's invitation to drink his blood should itself be proof that his sacrifice at that stage was not yet expiatory. By tradition, in an atonement sacrifice, the high priest sprinkled the victim's blood both before and upon the mercy seat of God. This attested, as it were, that the victim had been put to death, and the wages of sin duly paid, and sin ostensibly expiated. In Jesus's own case as an atonement sacrificial victim, his blood upon his death was to be smeared by the nails in his feet and wrists, and sprinkled by the plunging of the legionnaire's lance in his side, on and around the foot of the cross, which had now become the mercy seat.

Under no circumstances whatever was blood, let alone the blood of an atonement sacrifice, offered to its beneficiaries for any purpose, least of all to drink. The drinking of such a victim's blood would be extremely abhorrent, and would be tantamount to reimbibing sin. Because of all this, it seems evident that drinking Jesus's blood at the Last Supper could not have been drinking expiatory blood, whatever else it might have been.

If Jesus's blood at the Last Supper was not the blood of atonement or expiation, what was it then? And why was Jesus able to offer it as a potion in seemingly flagrant contravention of the prohibition against consuming blood?

Although it was his body, flesh, and blood that he offered as the sacrificial bearer of our sins, throughout John 6:51–56, it was his *flesh* that he offered for eating and his *blood* for drinking. As to his blood, all he proclaimed it to be at this juncture was the sealer of his covenant by which he had just offered his body to be carrier of our sins. "This cup is the new covenant in my blood which is being poured out *(ekchynnomenon)* on your account." With the chalice, he was offering us the means of our ratification of his new covenant. Our ratification is essential to our ordinary participation in the fruit of his covenant. Ordinarily, unless we eat of his flesh and drink of his blood, we would not be eucharistically saved. Our salvation would in that case have to be by a separate extraordinary act of grace.

A covenant is not itself a sacrifice, but a solemn agreement for mutual performance. The purpose of Jesus's covenantal blood was to bind parties together in a performance relationship. There is a well-known example of the use of covenantal blood in Exodus 24:1–11, when Moses recited the words and ordinances of the Lord to the assembled people. With one voice, the people exclaimed: "All the words that the Lord has spoken, we will do, and obey." The young men then sacrificed offerings of well-being to the Lord, and Moses sprinkled a portion of the blood on the people to indicate their ratification of the covenant between them and the Lord. On his part, the Lord undertook to cherish the Israelites above all peoples, and to install them as a kingdom of priests and a holy nation (Exodus 19:5–6).

In a similar vein, in the presence of the participants at the Last Supper, Jesus offered a covenantal relationship with the whole world, in which he would assume the sins of the entire world in his own person. This is the covenant of which John the Baptist was prophesied to be the messenger, the covenant of the *forgiveness* or remission of sins preached by him (Mark 1:4, Luke 3:3). Jesus's blood at the Last Supper was not *expiating* anything yet. At that stage, it only sealed his new covenant with us. In this covenant, it was up to us to seek and accept forgiveness of sins, but it was wholly up to him to atone for the sins thus forgiven. Like Moses's earlier covenant, Jesus's covenant stood in need of acceptance and ratification by us, the other party; and, like Moses, Jesus offered a method of covenantal ratification. As with Moses, the ratification involved the blood of the sacrificial victim. In the present case, the victim was Jesus himself, hence the covenantal blood had to be his own.

While Moses only sprinkled the blood of the victim on the Israelites, Jesus, the presenter of this new covenant, offered the blood of the victim, his own, as a potion to be drunk in a libation setting, and in that way signal our acceptance of this new covenant. That blood simply sealed this new covenant with those who would knowingly partake of it, a covenant that we enter into for the remission of our sins through Jesus's transferring them onto his own person. Our corresponding obligation, once we have confessed (i.e., acknowledged our sins), and repented (i.e., shown a willingness to let go of them and cease husbanding them), is to express our belief and trust in Jesus by living according to his injunction to love one another. Loving one another becomes here an expression of our kinship in common by our adoption through Jesus. The ostensible dilemma for us, however, is that there was no Judaic tradition of *drinking* blood, even as the sealer of a covenant.

Hence there arises the question of how Jesus could offer blood, especially his own blood, to anyone to drink in the land of Judea. Would that not have been an abomination? The eating of human flesh and the drinking of any blood were both abominations under Torah. When, teaching at the Capernaum synagogue earlier on, Jesus first broached the idea of the eating of his flesh and the drinking of his blood to his audience, he had, not surprisingly, caused the majority of his listeners to depart (John 6:48–66). Would Jesus's new covenant actually require his followers to break the law and commit an abomination in their process of ratifying his covenant? Had not Jesus himself stressed to the Baptist the necessity of observing law?

Accordingly, the wine that Jesus consecrated at the Last Supper, and pronounced to be his own blood, would not have possessed the empirical properties of human blood, but only those of wine, and mutatis mutandis for the unleavened bread, which he pronounced to be his flesh.

What, then, was the upshot, the illocutionary force, of such pronouncements as the words of institution? The transformation of the eucharistic wine into the blood of Christ does not involve a chemical or alchemical transmutation. The aim is not to secure an identity of substance between the wine and the blood of Christ, or the bread and the flesh of Christ, each of which would simply be a naturalistic conversion with no declared soteriological aim. Instead, the aim is fully to bestow upon the otherwise natural wine and bread a power and efficacy that otherwise belongs only to the blood and flesh of Christ. Christ promised to return and be present in the midst of those gathered in his name. Accordingly, when during the celebration of the Mass the priest prays for the transformation of the bread and wine, and utters the words of consecration, Christ, who is present, bestows upon the wine and the bread that sanctifying and salvific charism that is otherwise exclusive to his own blood and flesh. This alone is what makes the consecrated wine the blood of Christ, and the consecrated bread the body of Christ, an identity occurring not in the kingdom of nature but in the kingdom of grace.

The actual chemistry of the wine and the bread is not affected in the least. What is new is their dynamism. This, indeed, seems to be Jesus's point when he links the eating of his flesh and the drinking of his blood with our possibility of salvation, when he says that unless one eats his flesh and drinks his blood, one does not have life in oneself (John 6:53 NRSV). With the words of institution, Jesus Christ bestows the same power and efficacy on the consecrated bread and wine, a power and efficacy that immediately becomes transformative of them. It is this transformation in power and efficacy, rather than a transformation in their substance, that is the intent of those words.

When Jesus changed water into wine at the marriage feast at Cana, the water-become-wine did not continue to taste or look like water, but drew favorable comment as excellent wine. The aim of the words of institution, though, is not a similar change in substance, but that bread and wine should present that salvific charism that is exclusive to the flesh and blood of Jesus Christ

Aristotelian accidents—generally, those changeable features of an object that we know by our senses, together with its circumstances of space, time, and location—are indicators of the sort of object it is. Thus, the accidents of bread and wine are simply those features that make us recognize them as bread and wine. These so-called Aristotelian accidents are, of course, not haphazardly connected with the objects, and the indicators of flesh and blood would not appear to us like those of bread and wine even after consecration; nor would the flesh and blood of Jesus Christ actually swap indicators so as, by some degradation, to masquerade in the guise of bread and wine.

The stunning difference between consecrated wine and bread and all unconsecrated wine and bread is that at the moment Jesus pronounced the bread and wine to be his body and blood, they, concurrently with the pronouncement, became different from all unconsecrated wine and bread by becoming endued with a potency and an efficaciousness, a redemptive charism otherwise belonging only to the flesh and blood of Jesus. It is in just this and nothing else that transubstantiation can consist. Exactly the same radical change happens whenever a priest ordained in the apostolic succession properly pronounces the same words of institution. Consecration radically transforms bread and wine by bestowing on them a power and efficacy not possessed by bread or wine, but possessed only by the body and blood of Jesus Christ. This does not deny transubstantiation; it explicates it.

This new salvific potency and efficacy now belonging to the consecrated wine and bread are indeed discernible, while not by the faculties of sight or taste, certainly by that of faith, that very same inner faculty through which the attending apostles themselves discerned Jesus's flesh and blood in the consecrated bread and wine that they consumed at the Last Supper. Paul confesses that it is only spiritually that such discernment can occur (1 Corinthians 2:14). Since the charism is not itself spatio-temporal, it can be simultaneously effective in consecrated bread and wine, wherever they may be, without constraint of space or time or number, wherever and whenever the words of institution are properly affirmed.

This clarifies and regularizes the offering of Jesus's blood as a covenantal drink. It is because the consecrated wine, which now possesses all the salvific efficaciousness and potency of the blood of Christ, still retains the full panoply of the physical properties of grape wine that Jesus was able to present it and offer it as the ratifying drink of his covenant, without setting off an abomination. Only wine that has thus become charismatically identical with the blood of Christ, the victim, could, by our imbibing it, signal our acceptance of Jesus's new covenant. It is only in this way that we can actually "discern" the body and blood of Jesus in the consecrated bread and wine, as Paul demands.

Similar locutions are employed by Jesus at other times. When Jesus said to John, "Behold your mother" and to his own mother, "Woman, behold your son," even though they at once became mother and son, Jesus did not intend or perform a genetic conversion, only a dynamic, functional one. It is the same when he proclaims his brothers and sisters to be those who do the will of his father. He brings about a real change in moral being, but not a genetic transmutation.

In our own conscious partaking of the covenantal blood of Jesus at communion, we are affirming this charism and are asking him to bind us in his covenant for the transfer of our sins to him, and for their inclusion in his yet-to-come expiatory action on the cross at Golgotha. His eucharistic body unbinds us from our sins, and his eucharistic blood covenantally binds us to the atonement on the cross.

CHAPTER 7

WHY JESUS STILL HAD TO DIE ON THE CROSS

If Jesus's self-sacrifice really took place at the Last Supper, why did he have to go on to the cross and die? The fact is that, thus far, Jesus had only assumed our sins. While those sins had in consequence been forgiven to us, they had not yet been expiated by him. As we all very well know, sin forgiven is not sin forgotten. All that its forgiveness removes from us is responsibility for its expiation. As responsibility for expiating sins had by no means been quashed, this responsibility now lay squarely on Jesus, for he had not borne our sins in a merely figurative manner. He truly bore them in his own person, where they cried out for expiation. That cry for expiation caused Jesus to go on and die on the cross.

Even though Jesus assumed sins globally, it was individually that they were expiated. Moreover, had he simply forgiven them individually during the Last Supper, all of us would still have been liable to everlasting death for every further unconfessed, unforgiven, and all unexpiated sin. None of us would have had a path to everlasting life, which was actually the life that Jesus wanted to make available to us, his self-described life in abundance, or unending life. The way God revealed his love to us was to send his Son as expiation for our sins (1 John 4:10). To accomplish this, it was necessary first of all for his Son to take over our sins voluntarily, and then pay the price not only of the extant sins that he had taken over but also of those sins that would be committed in later ages; and, second, for him to overcome the eventual upshot of all sin, namely, uninterrupted death. Jesus's passion, or agony, which culminated in his death on the cross, was his means of expiating the sins for which he had assumed full responsibility at the Last Supper.

As to the Mass of the Last Supper itself, it occurred in the setting of the meal of the Passover lamb, which had not really been completed in all of its customary stages when Jesus and his disciples left for the garden of Gethsemane.

In current instructions for observances of the occasion, four cups of red wine were stipulated as part of the annual Passover meal of the lamb. Two cups were shared during the actual eating of the lamb. The remaining two cups were postprandial. These two were known, respectively, as the cup of redemption and the cup of consummation. The sharing of the cup of redemption celebrated God's fulfillment of his promise to redeem his people from the bondage of Egyptian slavery (Exodus 6:6f). The cup that Jesus offered after supper in his new covenant, the cup of the Mass, corresponded to that third cup, the cup of redemption, and offered us redemption from the slavery of sin. With it, Jesus declared a new covenantal relationship with the world, by which he offered us redemption from the bondage of our sins by taking them over himself. After this, he and his party left for Gethsemane, with the fourth cup, the cup of consummation, not yet served or shared.

Jesus's departure for Gethsemane did not signal the omission of the fourth cup. The fact is that that fourth cup could not yet be served by the fulfiller of God's promise of salvation, for he had not yet completed or *consummated* his salvific acts in this greatly expanded celebration. That cup could only be drunk during Jesus's final moments on the cross, near the point of his atoning death, at the verge of the resurrection, when God's promise to take his people to be with him would be validated. For it is only with the severance of the link between sin and everlasting death, achieved through Jesus's own resurrection, that we can have hopes of dwelling with God forever. Jesus had said: "And I, when I am lifted up from the earth, will draw all people to myself" (John 12:32 NRSV), meaning not lifted in his crucifixion, which was simply the instrument of his death, and hardly a propitious setting for drawing all people unto himself, but rather lifted up at his ascension following his resurrection into life. Indeed, it is only with his ascension that he can go and prepare a place for us, so that where he is, there will also be all who do his bidding (John 12:26 NRSV). This is a statement of the fullness of Jesus's covenant with us. We become his brethren, his brothers and sisters, when we do his will and the will of his Father, in virtue of which we can be where he was going to be. It would not be time to drink the cup of the consummation of salvation until Jesus was sacrificed on the cross, for only then could expiation be achieved. It was only with the expiation of sins, followed by the resurrection and ascension of Christ, that God's will to gather his people to dwell with him could come to fruition.

Even so, during the crucifixion, unseasonable attempts were made to serve Jesus this wine, and he refused it—the schedule was to be set by him, and not by his uninformed executioners. Accordingly, when the time was right, Jesus signaled it by inviting the cup with his declaration: "I thirst." As soon as he received the wine presented to him, he affirmed with magnificence the conclusion of his salvific acts: "It is accomplished," or consummated (John 19:28–30 NRSV). He had just taken the cup of consummation. He could now expire, paying for it all. From then on, the sins that he had assumed would no longer be in force or have any purchase. All the atoning sacrifices of the temple were now given full efficacy, fulfilled once and for all, in Jesus's own atoning death.

What did take place at the crucifixion was, objectively, the final act in the shedding of expiatory blood, an action that was set in train by the capital sentence decided by Caiaphas and confirmed by his Sanhedrin, and which culminated in the crucifixion. That crucifixion was obviously not perpetrated by Jesus himself, even though he had been the high priest at the Mass of the Last Supper. At the crucifixion, however, he was only the original and, hence, now compromised but continuing sacrificial victim, and could not now be the officiant on account of his new physical condition. The officiant retains his seal throughout the sacrifice, and, as to the sacrificial victim, it undergoes several regressive stages with the progress of the sacrifice. The officiant at this point was still Caiaphas, who had initiated the process when he originally designated Jesus as a sacrificial victim, but would be forced by Judaic law and tradition to delegate the actual slaying to Pontius Pilate and his soldiers, as Jesus had several times foretold. How this was achieved is the discussion of the next chapter.

CHAPTER 8

THE REASON FOR THE GENTILE INVOLVEMENT IN THE CRUCIFIXION

How did the Romans come to be involved in this, and would not their robust participation have vitiated what was, after all, a Jewish sacrifice? Executions carried out by Judeans were certainly not unknown. In fact, several extrajudicial attempts had been made on Jesus's own life, notably at his own Nazareth when he intimated that he was personally the fulfiller of Isaiah's messianic prophecy (Luke 4:16–30; also John 8:59, 10:31–32, 11:8). Similarly, zealous people had been ready, spurred on by scribes and Pharisees, to stone to death a woman allegedly surprised in flagrante delicto, until Jesus intervened to save her life (John 8:2–11). Why then did Caiaphas's own forces and the people at large not carry out Jesus's execution after the Sanhedrin had passed official sentence on him, thereby bolstering Caiaphas's determination to have Jesus sacrificed for the good of the nation?

Had Jesus been executed by Jewish forces, his death would not have been a valid sacrificial ransom on account of the Jewish proscription against human sacrifice. Quite apart from that Jewish proscription, in that year AD 33, there also existed a juridical impediment, for, in that very year, the Roman administration had abrogated the power of the high priest, the Sanhedrin, and Judeans in general to order, exact, or carry out any capital punishment anywhere in their land. This fact, cited by Caiaphas before Pilate (John 18:31), is also attested in Jerusalem Talmud (Sanhedrin 18a, 24b) and, reportedly, by Philo.

Jesus, of course, already knew, and several times remarked, that his own slaying would be carried out not by Jews, but by people who were not subject to Torah, thereby rendering those dual impediments of no consequence with regard to the completion of his mission. Close to his Passion, he declared that much to his apostles. Thus, at the inception of his final journey to Jerusalem, he said to them: "See, we are going up to Jerusalem, and the Son of Man will be handed over to the chief priests and scribes, and they will condemn him to death; then they will hand him over to the Gentiles to be mocked and flogged and crucified" (Matthew 20:18–19 NRSV; also Mark 10:33). On the third foretelling in Luke (18:32 NSRV), he said, "he will be handed over to the Gentiles; and he will be mocked and insulted and spat upon. After they have flogged him, they will kill him." At Matthew 26:45 (NRSV), he said while in the garden of Gethsemane: "See, the hour is at hand, and the Son of Man is being betrayed into the hands of sinners." At other places, "Enough! The time has come. See the Son of Man is being betrayed into the hands of sinners."

Peter, in the course of his own expatiation, said to his audience (Acts 2:23): "This man was arrested in accordance with God's predetermined plan and foreknowledge; and through the agency of men not bound by the Law, you nailed him up to the cross and killed him." Of course, in all such contexts, the term "sinners," like "Gentiles," was meant to designate not transgressors of the law, but people who were not at all subject to it, or, in Peter's words, people who were not bound by it, and consequently could not be said to infringe any of it; in other words, all who were not members of Jewish households, more or less the entire complement of non-Jews.

It is indeed clear, on account of the interdiction of human sacrifice, that Judeans would not have been able to complete by their own hands the ritual sacrifice of that Lamb of God. It is just as clear because of the Roman exclusion that Jesus could not have been juridically slain by Jewish hands in that year of AD 33. For that year then, it was quite unavoidable that Jesus, the sacrificial Lamb of God, be slain by Gentile hands, if at all possible. In full knowledge that he and his Sanhedrin were precluded under both divine law and secular decree from carrying out the ritual execution of Jesus necessary for the sacrifice, Caiaphas and his Sanhedrin were thus snagged between the horns of a dilemma.

Further complicating matters was the fact that Gentiles were not even permitted to proffer a ransom or atonement sacrifice to God, much less slay one. How, then, could Jesus's execution by agents who were not subject to Judaic law and tradition have been part of God's plan to ransom sinners, and why would such agency not have caused the derailment of a sacrifice that was proposed by the high priest as a ransom for the nation? Would a prominent Gentile participation be ritually permissible?

Through resort to casuistry and complicated maneuvers, Caiaphas and his Sanhedrin would eventually achieve their goal of securing the sacrifice of Jesus to God, who is the recipient of all Jewish sacrifices, as a human ransom, while at the same time observing every particular of their own law and tradition.

Under Judean law and tradition, animal sacrifices were not always slaughtered by the high priest himself, nor by other sacerdotal assistants. On Yom Kippur, however, and on solemn occasions like that of the Passover of the Lamb, and especially during the Feast of Unleavened Bread, the high priest was under a legal obligation to be in attendance not only on those specified days themselves, but also on each day of their preceding week. At other times, however, sacrifices could be validly slain by a layman, or the person or people presenting the animals for sacrifice. On Passover of the Lamb day, especially, people slaughtered their own lambs on the temple grounds, while formations of priests from all twenty-four divisions, or courses, lined up in two rows and collected the blood in gold and silver basins. Each presenter skinned his own lamb and removed the fat and kidneys for burning at the altar. He then muffled the carcass in its skin, and carried it home for the preparation of the Passover meal.

Slaying could even be carried out by non-Jews, although such persons would need to have been circumcised in order to be permitted within the temple precincts by stipulation of Ezekiel 44:7–9. Gentile temple participation, however, excluded sin-offerings, trespass-offerings, and purification-offerings, for those presupposed infringement of accepted laws of God, and so were permissible only to those fully subject to those laws.

This restriction applied without exception to all Gentiles, whether proselyte or nonproselyte. Acceptable from Gentiles were gifts and free-will offerings, and these became quite extensive on account of the considerable and widespread renown of the Jerusalem sanctuary. Josephus states that Lucius Vitellius, the governor of Syria, who ordered Pontius Pilate back to Rome to answer charges about the slaughter of Samaritans at Mount Gerizim (the very man who also subsequently deposed Caiaphas from the high priesthood in favor of Jonathan, son of the former high priest Ananias) did come to Jerusalem during Passover in AD 37 in order to offer a sacrifice to God, and had been received on the friendliest of terms (Josephus, Jewish Antiquities, 18.5.3).

In the present case, however, where the sacrificial offering was actually to be a human being, and a Judean at that, no Judean, whether high priest, sacerdotal assistant, or lay, even if improbably personally without sin, would have been able to carry out the slaying. This was on account of the prescript against human sacrifice. What the Sanhedrin needed in order to achieve the physical slaying of Jesus was not merely a Gentile agent, but a Gentile agent who could do so within the trammels of the law and tradition.

As a matter of fact, it was to a very Gentile administration, the Roman administration in the person of Pontius Pilate, that God himself had accorded the power of life and death over Jesus. This was revealed when Pilate told Jesus that he did have an original authority, and Jesus had disabused his mind of that fantasy by informing him: "You would have no such authority over me at all if it had not been given you from above" (John 9:10–11 NRSV). Even though Caiaphas would find his man, there would still be certain steps that needed to be followed before that special authority of Pilate's could be deployed.

At the time when Jesus began his mission, the Jewish national expectation, outside of the band of those expecting simply a teacher of righteousness, was that the Messiah would, like Moses of old, perform such stupendous signs and wonders as would irrefutably establish his credentials and prowess. Jesus personally indulged that expectation when he cryptically announced to those Pharisees and Sadducees who had come to test him by demanding a sign from heaven (Matthew 16:1), that the only sign he would vouchsafe seekers-after-signs would be the sign of Jonah (verse 4): entombment and reemergence, entering the womb and being born again, destroying (t)his temple and raising it up on the third day! To top his previous well-known wonders, he fatefully called forth to life Lazarus, who had been dead for some three days (John 11:17–19, 39 NRSV). This feat garnered for Jesus a considerable added following (11:45, 12:10). Little did anyone know, however, that Jesus's own intended sign, hinted at but darkly, would be the most stupendous imaginable: a self-resurrection on the third day of death and entombment! Impressive as such a sign was bound to be, that allusion to his own death, however, only promoted mystification among his audience: for they had generally believed that, according to messianic lore, the expected Christ was to enjoy uninterrupted life (John 12:34) in his single parousia.

According to John 11:38–53, it was after Jesus raised Lazarus that some of the Judeans, who had come to mourn with Mary and Martha over the death of their brother, Lazarus, went off to the tormented Pharisees with stories of that disquieting accomplishment. Upon being informed, the chief priests and Pharisees convoked the Sanhedrin, and that was where Caiaphas, under inspiration (verse 51) as high priest, first proposed officially that Jesus be sacrificed to die on behalf of the nation (verses 49, 50).

The Sanhedrin's calculation was that, capping Jesus's previous miracles, the raising of Lazarus would be sure to increase his following and cause the populace to look more to Jesus for guidance than to themselves, their established leaders, and possibly even cause them to embrace Jesus's unconventional ways and relaxed practices. In that calculation, they were actually correct. Many of the witnesses carried news of the miracle back home, and throngs would soon be descending upon Jerusalem for the looming festival of the Passover of Unleavened Bread. People would gather both on its first day and on its last day, in the hope of seeing not only Jesus but also the now famous Lazarus (11:56, 12:9) among the crowds at one or other of the two scheduled gatherings. The world was indeed rapidly turning toward Jesus (12:19).

The Sanhedrin's greatest apprehension was that the Romans, who as a rule brought in sizable contingents of soldiers to Jerusalem around Passover, could be provoked into bearing down hard on, and in the end destroying, the Sanhedrin and the nation itself (11:48). It is really quite understandable that in all of this, Caiaphas should seem particularly frantic, for, after all, it was a Roman, Valerius Gratus, the procurator predecessor of Pontius Pilate, who had chosen and installed him high priest, and his tenure as high priest thus rested on Roman sufferance.

From that day on, the Sanhedrin mulled over plans to have Jesus executed (verse 53). On catching wind of this conspiratorial meeting and its outcome, Jesus promptly retreated to the town of Ephraim in the desert region.

The time of greatest danger for all concerned would be that coming Passover Festival of Unleavened Bread in Jerusalem, when Jesus himself should be expected to be present in public, as should also the concentration of his many disciples and countless admirers. Not a few of them would be driven by sheer curiosity to see the man who stunningly resuscitated a putrefying corpse after days of entombment (verses 17–19) and, indeed, also Lazarus himself, the man returned from the dead (John 12:9). There was no telling what the very extraordinary Jesus or his ardent admirers might do. Accordingly, the Sanhedrin resolved to kill not only Jesus but Lazarus also, that involuntary instigator of the swarm (12:10). While delay might seem imprudent, at the same time, even a stealthy but precipitous move against Jesus at either of the two mandated convocations would carry its own peril. An uproar of the people would be all too likely (Matthew 26:5, Mark 14:2, Luke 22:2).

Committed now on grounds of national security to the slaying of Jesus as a sacrifice for the nation, Caiaphas was still to find it impossible to proceed unless he could first secure the acquiescence and cooperation of two groups, namely, the same Judean populace that had become increasingly enamored of Jesus, and the Roman administration, without whose collaboration Jesus could not be executed at all. Otherwise Caiaphas would provoke, through an arrant act of insubordination, that same vigorous Roman reaction that he seemed to be going to murderous lengths to forestall.

As to the general populace, it was not as if Caiaphas lacked real and momentous grievances against Jesus, grievances not connected with statecraft, yet capable of aiding him in his homicidal course of action. Had not Jesus forcibly disrupted regular commerce on the temple grounds, commerce organized by the priests and from which they derived sizable incomes? Such interference was in itself a capital offense. As far as that went, though, the general populace would probably side with Jesus in his disruption of the den of thieves and its profiteering commercial activities on the grounds of the temple, the house of God. Beyond that, however, Jesus was under suspicion of having spoken sacrilegiously about the temple, site of the Holy of Holies, when he seemed to vaunt that if the temple was destroyed, he could personally rebuild that temple of God within three days! Some other witnesses were even prepared to claim that Jesus had threatened to destroy with his own hands that edifice built with human hands, and replace it in three days with another not built with human hands at all.

Grim as those were, in the end such charges would hardly have countervailed Jesus's exalted standing in the minds of the people who were disposed to proclaim him king of Israel, especially not after what he had freshly done for Lazarus. The only way Caiaphas could hope to secure the acquiescence of the populace would be to prefer against Jesus charges that everyone would be bound to recognize as meriting death upon conviction. Such charges would have to be religious and ecclesiastical, such as an attack on the high priest or blasphemy against God's majesty, but Jesus had never attacked the person of the high priest by word or by deed, nor had he ever blasphemed God's majesty.

Jesus himself was in the end to lend Caiaphas a hand in his quest. As the supreme judicial, religious, and ecclesiastical body of the nation, the Sanhedrin was the only body that could give formal sanction to Caiaphas's plan. Caiaphas marveled at Jesus's reticence during his appearance before the Sanhedrin, just as Pilate would later marvel at a similar reticence in the face of what many biased witnesses had been alleging against him (Matthew 26:60, 62, 63; Mark 14:60–61). Managing his own Passion, Jesus was waiting for just that one charge, the charge of blasphemy, which would inevitably earn him the sentence of death. In response to Caiaphas's direct question before the Sanhedrin, "Are you the Messiah, the Son of the Blessed One?" Jesus offered an equally direct answer: "I am; and you will see the Son of Man seated at the right hand of the Power, and 'coming with the clouds of heaven'" (Mark 14:61–62 NRSV; and also Matthew 26:63–66; Luke 22:67–71). With that provocative response, the die was cast, and the resulting charge of blatant blasphemy would seem able to mollify those enthusiastic admirers who had only days before heaped encomiums on Jesus as he rode into Jerusalem.

Blasphemy against God would ordinarily be punishable by stoning, followed by hanging on a tree for the rest of the day, and burial in an "ignominous" and "obscure" manner (Jewish Antiquities, 4.8.6). The Sanhedrin formally endorsed the charge and unanimously pronounced the sentence of death.

Clear that there at last was a way to pacify the populace, Caiaphas was now faced with only two impediments: the Judean lack of legal power to carry out the capital sentence and the requirement of carrying it out as a ransom sacrifice, which would be within Judaic law and tradition.

The chief priests and elders entered into deliberation on how to resolve both conundrums so that Jesus could actually be put to death (Matthew 27:1). They devised a complex plan to maneuver the Roman authorities into cooperating. That plan consisted in inducing the Roman authorities to make the execution of Jesus their own cause. The Sanhedrin had already decided to involve Roman soldiers, acting in collusion with temple guards in Jesus's arrest, with the aim no doubt of discouraging possible public interference. To entangle the Romans even more securely, the Sanhedrin would frame fresh charges that the Romans would be bound to acknowledge as warranting death. Such a charge would have to be political in order to move the Romans at all; in fact, a charge of subversion and sedition. They now bound Jesus the last time (Matthew 27:2), and delivered him to Pilate in the opening gambit of their complex scheme.

A feinting appeal to Pontius Pilate on the score that Jesus had quite blasphemously called himself the Son of God and must die (John 19:7 and Matthew 27:12–14), the accusations by the chief priests and elders, and the many things they testified against him: to all of these, and to Pilate's great amazement, Jesus offered no response (also Mark 15:2–5 and Luke 23:14).

On this occasion, the charge Jesus was waiting for was that of sedition (the dreaded *seditio* of the Romans), that he had nominated himself the Messiah of prophecy, and accordingly the redoubtable king of the Jews who would restore sovereignty to the nation. This was the charge to which Pilate should be expected to react wholeheartedly. Initially eyeing Jesus, Pilate had not considered his physical appearance and taciturn demeanor characteristic of a plausible insurgent, and was inclined to dismiss the charge as not credible. As to the religious accusations—"the many things they testified against him"—he exhorted the Sanhedrin to take care of their own religious disputes. On account of the regard with which many Judeans held Jesus, unlike the Sanhedrin itself (Mark 15:10), Pilate was aware that the religious charges might have been triggered by resentment and jealousy. Forearmed, Caiaphas was quick to respond somewhat reproachfully that it was not lawful for them to put anyone to death (John 18:31).

It was brilliant of Caiaphas and his Sanhedrin to have framed the complaint to Pontius Pilate initially in religious terms, because their relentless desire to have Jesus executed soon led Pontius Pilate to believe that there might exist a grave and compelling pious indictment of Jesus. It might also have impelled Pilate to have misgivings about the original wisdom of trimming Sanhedrin judicial and executive power, if he himself was not to become embroiled in Judaic religious disputes, which, if left unresolved, could lead to turmoil and riots. That could have been why capital authority was restored to the Sanhedrin in the very next year AD 34, thus enabling the unwavering Jerusalem authorities to order and carry out Stephen's execution by stoning, the murder of other salient disciples of Jesus, and subsequently the apostle James himself, whereas until then they had largely had to be content with the arrest and imprisonment of Jesus's followers.

As to the wily Caiaphas, it may be doubted whether he really regretted the limits placed on the power of the Sanhedrin in the present case. For that matter, he and his colleagues would hardly have felt confident about putting to death by their own hands a man whom practically the whole of Jerusalem had only days before acclaimed as their king and Messiah, for they dreaded the likely popular reaction, and had even been full of qualms about snatching Jesus at either of the two massively attended public assemblies of the people during the Passover Festival of Unleavened Bread (Exodus 12:6). Not on the feast day, they said, in full fear of their causing an uproar among the people (Mark 14:2, Matthew 26:5).

No similar public assembly was commanded for the Passover of the Lamb, which could therefore be expected to provide a less public opportunity and more discreet cover for the arrest. In the end, Jesus's arrest did take place in seclusion and in the dark at the garden of Gethsemane, hours before midnight when the temple gates were to be thrown open to public gatherings, as they customarily were following the eating of the Passover lamb, on the first of the feast days of Unleavened Bread (Jewish Antiquities, 18.2.2).

In searching for a complaint that would be indictable under Roman law and would carry the death penalty, Caiaphas readily found it in the events surrounding Jesus's entry into Jerusalem. When Jesus was riding into Jerusalem earlier in the week, crowds were spreading fronds and twigs on the ground ahead of him, singing "Hosanna" to this son of David, and chanting things such as, "Blessed is he who is coming in the name of the Lord," "the king of Israel himself," "Blessed is the king of Israel who is coming in the name of the Lord," "Hosanna in the highest places" (Matthew 21:9, 15; Mark 11:9–10; John 12:13). Jesus himself confirmed his regal status when he responded to demurrers that the very stones would take up the identical paean, were the crowd to be silenced. Besides, by his very mode of arrival he brought to pass yet another messianic prophecy relating to his kingship (Zechariah 9:9, Zephaniah 3.15). Of considerable interest to the Romans would be both the designation of Jesus as king of Israel, and the liberation exhortation "Hosanna!" which meant "Liberate us right now!" and was in the present context purely political. In its original context (Psalm 118:25), the cry for liberation was also coupled with an urgent plea to send prosperity now. Even so, Pilate was not fully convinced that everything was aboveboard.

Religious history was on Pilate's side. Soon after the Torah was fixed and became the Book of the Law when Ezra was scribe, intense study of the law began, and that led to a burgeoning both of rabbis to expound and teach the law and of synagogues in which to teach it. Progressively, the people began to rely for guidance more on rabbis than on priests, and sacrifices began to play second fiddle to the learning of the law and its observance. This trend was at its height at the time of Jesus's own ministry, and he himself felt the need to admonish the people to hearken to the scribes and Pharisees, and practice and observe whatever they instruct (though not what they do) because they sit on Moses's seat, and so represent the Mosaic magisterium. Jesus was hardly thereby endorsing the content of their teaching or the law in this its Halakhah form, for he condemned provisions of it. They tie up heavy burdens hard to bear and lay them on the shoulders of others (Matthew 23:4); they say whoever swears by the sanctuary is bound by nothing but whoever swears by the gold of the sanctuary is bound by the oath. They are blind fools who think the gold on the sanctuary is greater than the sanctuary that sanctifies the gold (23:17)! They blindly say whoever swears by the altar is bound by nothing, but whoever swears by the gift on the altar is bound by his oath, not seeing that it is the altar that makes the gift on it sacred! He was exhorting the people to obedience, which is what the Judaic law demanded. It is the same sort of force inherent in decisions of the US Supreme Court or the British Privy Council. They demand compliance but are hardly beyond criticism.

Now, Jesus himself was not known to have been schooled at the feet of any of the rabbis (John 7:14–16). Consequently, with his meteoric rise as an unaffiliated yet authoritative teacher (Matthew 7:29; Mark 1:22, 27; Luke 4:32), who frequently reproved traditional rabbis and priests alike, priests and rabbis could think that history was in the process of repeating itself. Rabbis and priests would seek an alliance with chief priests to portray Jesus as a dangerous upstart. This may be why Pilate sensed that there was considerable envy mixed with fear in the arrest of Jesus. As far as the Roman imperium itself was concerned, though, Jesus had seemed quite tolerant of it, to the extent of advising his hearers to render unto Caesar the things that were Caesar's. Pilate seemed on the whole inclined to be kindly disposed toward Jesus.

Pilate was reinforced in his suspicions regarding the accusations when Herod Antipas, tetrarch of Galilee, who was in Jerusalem at that time in connection with the Passover, and to whom he had sent Jesus for consideration of the particulars, returned Jesus to him with no declaration of any capital offense (Luke 23:15). In the end, however, Pilate was to be pressured by the crowd into acquiescing, for they had by this time turned against Jesus simply on account of his conviction on the charges of sacrilege and blasphemy, which they understood to be capital offenses, and took very seriously indeed. They warned Pilate that if he did not condemn Jesus for sedition, he would be no friend of the emperor (to whom Pilate himself did owe his position). So clear to them was Jesus's conviction on the charge of blasphemy that it became easy for them to deflate Pilate with the blood cry of Matthew 27:25, with the declaration that Jesus's blood be on them and on their children!

And yet, in the grand scheme of things still hidden from Caiaphas, Jesus's execution would be a *religious* fulfillment, not a political stratagem. Caiaphas remained unaware of the doubl' entendre lurking in his own official pronouncement that it would be a good thing for Jesus to die for the sake of the nation (John 11:49f). Objectively, he had consigned the Lamb of God to death as a ransom for the nation, thereby designating him a sacrificial victim. In this, Caiaphas would not be pursuing a vendetta for the many reproofs flung at the chief priests and scribes and Pharisees by Jesus, though never against the high priest himself. Nor would he be seeking punishment for some other imagined crime or crimes committed. His was a high priest's designation of a sacrificial victim as ransom for the nation. As with all sacrificial victims, ironically, it implied Jesus's own personal innocence and spotlessness.

The ransom of the Judaic nation was, however, only the half of it. The actual power of that sacrifice was to ransom Jew and Gentile alike. In the words of 1 John 2:21, Jesus was not merely the propitiation for Jewish sins; he was actually the propitiation for the sins of the whole world.

In Peter's declaration (Acts 2:23), the man, Jesus, was arrested in accordance with God's predetermined plan and foreknowledge, the plan in question being the redemption of the world as a whole. In the necessary parts of that plan, it was for the Father, God, to place his seal of approval on Jesus as his sacrificial lamb; it was for the high priest to nominate Jesus as a ransom offering to God; and it was for the leading powers of the Judaic nation (the high priest and the Sanhedrin) as well as the in situ leading powers of the Gentiles (Pontius Pilate and his Roman administration) to collaborate in all of the Passion. That last part started with the joint arrest in Gethsemane by temple forces and a detachment of Roman troops, and came to a climax in the slaying of the Lamb of God, a ransom for both the Jewish nation (the nation under Torah) and the Gentile nations (all nations not under Torah). In all the world, there would be no bystanders at all, for there would be no beneficiaries who would not have had a hand in the necessity of the propitiatory sacrifice—and all are beneficiaries. All beneficiaries have a causal involvement in the sacrifice, and no one lot of beneficiaries would be required or be able to carry the burden of ensuring the expiatory sacrifice all by itself.

The Father and the Sanhedrin had done their part. It was only left for Gentiles to do their own part through their on-the-spot representatives. Accordingly, it was by a fiat of Pontius Pilate, representing all Gentiles, and by the hands of purely Gentile agents, that Jesus was duly slain in accordance with God's predetermined plan and foreknowledge. The Gentile role in this was the bloody and, thus, the culminating deed. Pontius Pilate, the Gentile who actually authorized the crucifixion by his soldiers, would not be able to retract the Gentile role by his manual ablutions.

The setup by which Caiaphas maneuvered Pilate and the Romans into putting Jesus to death brings up the question whether the Roman, thus Gentile, participation nullified the religious validity of the crucifixion in the context of a Jewish sacrifice. Obviously, this must be a moot question since that participation was an element in God's own plan. Even so, the rationale for it could still be educed.

That brings up the second reason, a ritual reason, why Caiaphas and the Sanhedrin needed Gentile involvement. Simply on account of the proscription against human sacrifice, only those who were not subject to the Law would be able to carry out the slaying of this sacrificial victim validly, provided only that the deed was in all other relevant respects carried out in consonance with Judaic law and tradition. This was the gravamen of Peter's declaration: "This man was arrested in accordance with God's predetermined plan and foreknowledge; and through the agency of men not bound by the Law you nailed him up on a cross and killed him!" Peter's reference to "men not bound by the Law" was an indication of the only procedure by which that sacrificial killing could be validly carried out.

Caiaphas and the deliberating Sanhedrin, with full knowledge of the Law and tradition, soon enough saw the same thing that Jesus had been foretelling. Without a doubt, from their own point of view, it seemed like a cunning artifice: get Gentiles without the Law to carry out the sacrificial killing (Matthew 27:1). The Romans were certainly uncircumcised, and prided themselves on that fact. If the victim has already been designated a ransom, as the high priest Caiaphas had done with Jesus, then the slaying of Jesus as ransom for the Jewish nation and non-Jewish nations could be validly carried out by delegation within Judaic law and tradition, (even by Gentiles, who, being Gentiles, were consequently not under Torah), provided only that the Gentiles themselves did not carry out the execution in the spirit of making a ransom or an atonement sacrifice, and provided also that the slaying took place outside the temple precincts and outside the city walls of Jerusalem. Hence the exurban Golgotha.

Jesus Christ himself, acting as high priest in the order of Melchizedek, had, with a view to making his slaying a ransom, ritually taken over our sins at the Mass of the Last Supper; for no other person could saddle Jesus with our sins, as the high priests had traditionally sought to saddle sacrificial animals with the sins of the people. The only one who as high priest could do this was Jesus Christ himself. As to the slaying of the victim, into which Jesus had now turned himself, that was not his responsibility at all, but the sole responsibility of the high priest Caiaphas, who had designated Jesus a sacrificial victim. It was therefore Caiaphas who had the responsibility of delegating the slaying of Jesus to Gentiles. It was through such scrupulous following of the Law that the slaying of Jesus was able to be a sacrifice with redeeming value and not sheer murder by non-Jews.

The messianic content of Pilate's own titulus on Jesus's cross, "King of the Jews," could not be overlooked, for it correctly identified the victim. Ironically, so had the mocking obeisance to "the King of the Jews" on the part of the Roman soldiers. Even so, given Pilate's character, his refusal to change the wording, and his easy release of the body, not to the chief priests, however, but to those who would grant it a decent burial, may be read as his attempt to have the last word after having been cowed into passing the death sentence. The Messiah, priest in the order of Melchizedek by virtue of his personal righteousness and king in the line of David by virtue of his mother, Mary, was Caiaphas's sacrificial victim and the nation's ransom, and, by his own will and the mercy of God, a ransom for the whole world. Caiaphas correctly felt assured that the ransom had been successfully paid.

The chief priests, the scribes, and general passers-by who taunted Jesus on the cross with invitations to step down if he was truly the Son of God, or to save himself as he had saved others, were trying him by ordeal, in fact challenging him to fulfill the sign of Jonah which he had said he would give them. The sign of Jonah did not even consist in a simple reemergence on the third day of entombment in a sea creature. Its promise was redemption following the repentance of the people of Nineveh, and their salvation from utter destruction. The promise of Jesus as a latter-day Jonah, writ large, was the remission of sins following repentance, their expiation, and accruing everlasting life.

CHAPTER 9

THE REAL MEANING OF "PREPARATION DAY"

The present account of the slaying of Jesus might have ended here but for a calendric discrepancy that is often alleged between the Synoptic Gospels and the fourth gospel. It relates to such a crucially significant issue as the date and day of the crucifixion of Jesus Christ. Most people are certain that it took place on what has come to be known as Good Friday; many scholars, however, believe that it took place on the preceding Thursday and before the Passover meal of the lamb could be eaten; a few even think that it had taken place on the preceding Wednesday! All base themselves on the testimony of the Gospels.

It would indeed be greatly astonishing if so momentous an incertitude had escaped the notice of Saint Augustine, one of whose major tasks was to establish the harmony of the Gospels. It would be utterly mind-numbing if this sort of discrepancy had been recognized by the early church, only to be ignored! It would boggle the mind even more if this discrepancy had managed to escape notice altogether. And yet that is what the calendric question would indicate. To my mind, it is wholly conclusive that Saint Augustine knew nothing at all of it and made no mention of it in his work, *The Harmony of the Gospels*. In chapter 13 of book three, Saint Augustine went to great pains to reconcile the apparent discrepancy between Mark (15:25) and John (19:14) as to the exact *hour* when Jesus's crucifixion became definitive. Would he have missed or ignored a discrepancy between the Synoptic Gospels and John's gospel as to the exact *day* of Jesus's crucifixion?

It can only be concluded that there had been no awareness of such a thing as a discrepancy as to the *day* when Jesus was crucified, the so-called calendric question. From this realization alone there should arise an impetus to take a look at this purely modern question and its actual context. The history and thesis in the present section are wholly derived from Jewish discussions of the chronology.

Passover is presented in Tanakh (the Hebrew Bible) as two distinct but interconnected and successive observances, the Passover of the Lamb and the Passover Feast of Unleavened Bread (e.g., Numbers 28:16–25, Deuteronomy 16:1–8, 2 Chronicles 35:7–9, 12). Curiously, throughout Tanakh, the Passover of the Lamb is never referred to as a feast (notwithstanding an unclear verse, viz. "You shall not offer the blood of my sacrifice with leaven, and the sacrifice of the festival of the passover shall not be left until the morning" (Exodus 34:25 NRSV), in contrast with the *feast* of Unleavened Bread, which is referred to under that rubric at least ten times. The same reserve can be observed in the Gospels in Greek (he heorte). The reason is probably that the Passover of the Lamb was intended as an *offering* to the Lord, whereas the Feast of Unleavened Bread was a thorough-going and protracted *festival in* the Lord's honor (Leviticus 23:5–6). When notice is taken of the fact that in verses 23 and 24 of Exodus 34, God is speaking of *three* feasts, it becomes extremely likely that the Paschal feast referred to in verse 25 is the Paschal Feast of Unleavened Bread, the two other feasts being the Feast of Weeks and the Feast of Tabernacles, these being the three feasts noted in Tanakh.

The slaughter of the Passover lamb and its preparation were mandated for 14 Nisan (Leviticus 23:5; Numbers 9:5, 28:16), and the preparation of the Passover Feast of Unleavened Bread from 15 Nisan for a whole week (Leviticus 23:6, Numbers 28:17).

By the morning of the day of the Passover of the Lamb, all Jewish homes would have been scoured for leavening, and all the leavened products that had not been incinerated would be consumed at breakfast that morning. By noon, whatever all twenty-four orders or divisions of priests and their assistants could confiscate during their previous night's searches would be consigned to flames on the temple grounds. That would enable the priests to declare the entire land of Judah, which was under their control, to be free of leavening before the preparation started in the afternoon. The scouring for leavening, like the correct preparation of the meal, was essential in Passover of the Lamb day observance, and was protected work, all *ordinary* work on that day being prohibited. After breakfast on 14 Nisan, the day of the Passover of the Lamb, and all through the weeklong Feast of Unleavened Bread, only unleavened bread could be eaten.

In the course of their checkered history, these two observances frequently fell into abeyance. Even after King Hezekiah (739–687 BC) had successfully restored them (2 Chronicles 30:1), they were still neglected for decades at a time until King Josiah (649–609 BC) more securely reinstituted them (2 Kings 23:23, 2 Chronicles 35:1), and merged them into one sustained celebration, the Feast of Unleavened Bread, swallowing the Passover of the Lamb. This is how they remained (e.g., Ezekiel 45:21) until the first century BC, when they were again separated into two sacred observances.

The two observances were still split at the time of Jesus (e.g., Mark 14:1) where clear reference is made to Passover and the Feast of Unleavened Bread. They indeed remained split throughout the New Testament period, and were so known to Josephus (e.g., Jewish Antiquities 3.10.5, 18.2.2). Though separate in identity, both the meal of the lamb and the Feast of Unleavened Bread were Pesach, Passover of the Lord (2 Chronicles 35:17, Ezekiel 45:21, Mark 14:1, Luke 22:1, 7). Thus, Luke 22:1 reports that the Feast of Unleavened Bread, which is called Passover, drew near.

Passover of the Lamb day in AD 33 began as usual at sunset on the preceding day; that is, the evening of Wednesday, 13 Nisan, and lasted till sunset on Thursday, 14 Nisan. Tanakh measures it as the period between the two evenings (Leviticus 23:5), night and day, as Jewish days were measured. It was on that very day that Jesus's disciples asked him where he would like to eat the sacred meal. Matthew 26:17 (NRSV) has: "On the first of the days of Unleavened Bread, the disciples came to Jesus, saying 'where do you want us to make preparations for you to eat the Passover?'" Mark 14:1 (NRSV), more informatively states: "On the first day of Unleavened Bread, when the Passover lamb is sacrificed, his disciples said to him, 'Where do you want us to go and make the preparations for you to eat the Passover?'" Luke 22:7–9 (NRSV), similarly attentive, records: "Then came the day of Unleavened Bread, on which the Passover lamb had to be sacrificed. So Jesus sent Peter and John, saying, 'Go and prepare the Passover meal for us that we may eat it.' They asked him, 'Where do you want us to make preparations for it?'" In response, Jesus instructed Peter and John to go to a predesignated host in the city, who would offer them all requisite resources (Luke 22:10–13). Peter and John were duly able to see to the completion of the preparations. Matthew 26:19–21 (NRSV) finishes the story: "So the disciples did as Jesus had directed them; and they prepared the passover meal. When it was evening, he took his place with the twelve; and while they were eating, he said ..."

Since unleavened bread is commanded with the eating of the Passover lamb, and, after breakfast on 14 Nisan, every home would in effect have been completely leaven free, it follows that "the first day of Unleavened Bread" is Passover of the Lamb day (14 Nisan) itself. It bears reiteration that the regimen of unleavened bread began right after breakfast that morning on Passover of the Lamb day. Hence, the day on which the Passover lamb was slaughtered, and not the first day of the Feast of Unleavened Bread, which is only the following day (15 Nisan), became recognized as the *first day* of unleavened bread (i.e., 14 Nisan). The unleavened bread eaten with the Passover lamb is, like the lamb itself, prepared on that Passover day.

The yearling lambs for the Passover meal were picked out on 10 Nisan, a good four days ahead of the meal's preparation on Passover of the Lamb day (Exodus 12:3–5). The lambs were then sheltered against all injury and misadventure, and were reexamined daily so that they would still be without blemish when they were presented for slaughter at the temple in the early afternoon of 14 Nisan, the day of the Passover of the Lamb. To gain admittance, the lambs were given their final inspection and received a seal of approval before being let in for slaughter. Presenters slaughtered their own lambs and skinned them, removing the fat and the kidneys for burning, while the blood was collected in golden and silver bowls by the priests for spattering at the altar. Practically all the chief priests would be in attendance at the temple. Each presenter rewrapped his animal in its skin and carried it home for roasting.

When the carcass was brought home, it was roasted whole over fire on a spit of pomegranate wood, for an estimated two hours for a thirty-pound lamb. It was served in due course with unleavened bread, bitter herbs, and red wine.

A different regimen applied to the next day, on which began the weeklong Feast of Unleavened Bread. On this and each of the other days of the seven-day-long Feast of Unleavened Bread, morning and evening sacrifices were slaughtered, and meat from those sacrifices was consumed with unleavened bread. The afternoon onward of the first and seventh days of the feast was a time of rest for all those not involved with the preparation of the meals. It would seem that it was the afternoon onward of that first day of the Feast of Unleavened Bread, which was referred to in John's gospel as the preparation day. The correct reason will be made clear later in this chapter.

Meanwhile, even if the designation *preparation day* were to be applied to the preparations for the meals, it would not only lucidly point up the afternoon business of its solemn day, but it would also serve to distinguish between the day of preparation and the day of eating of its sacred meal, which was always the day after, that is, after sunset. Thus, in Leviticus 23:5–6 (NRSV), "In the first month, on the fourteenth day of the month, at twilight, there shall be a passover offering to the Lord, and on the fifteenth day of the same month is the festival of unleavened bread to the Lord; seven days you shall eat unleavened bread." Thus also at Deuteronomy 16:6 (NRSV): "But at the place that the Lord your God will choose as a dwelling for his name, only there shall you offer the passover sacrifice, in the evening at sunset." We remember that each sunset began a new day.

So the Passover lamb in AD 33 was eaten only at day's end, after the sun had set on the day of the Passover of the Lamb; that would make it the beginning of Friday, 15 Nisan, the first day of the Feast of Unleavened Bread by the Hebrew calendar, though by our own Gregorian calendar it would have been Thursday night. All of this puts the Synoptic Gospels in consonance with one another. All three make Jesus's last supper a Passover of the Lamb meal.

It was night, well after the sun had set upon 14 Nisan, the day of the Passover of the Lamb, and now well into the initial hours of 15 Nisan, when Jesus and his disciples finished eating their final supper together.

In reality, however, the designation *preparation day* can have little to do with the preparation for the Passover of the Lamb meal. That preparation started four days earlier, with the selection of the yearling lamb, which was inspected daily for misadventures. On the night marking the beginning of the day of Passover of the Lamb, the preparation continued with the hunt for leaven, and the sheep would not be slaughtered till the afternoon of that day, a few hours before the day's end. No one day could be called a *preparation day* for it. A single meal that is to be eaten would simply need to be prepared on schedule, like a Sunday dinner. A Sunday dinner would certainly not merit a special preparation day, unless it was to be prepared before Sunday. No more would the Passover of the Lamb meal, whose preparation was mandated for the afternoon of its very day. As to the first meal of the Feast of Unleavened Bread, that too would simply be prepared on schedule on its first day, with no call for a specially named preparation day.

With the foregoing as background, an attempt can now be made to sort out the calendric question in its actual context. All four gospels, the Synoptic Gospels as well as the fourth gospel, are evidently in agreement as to the substance, even if, allegedly, not as to the timing, of the events of Jesus's entire Passion, from his distress in the garden of Gethsemane to his execution on the hill of Golgotha. They are also in agreement that Jesus had verifiably expired by midafternoon on Friday 15 Nisan—at a time, then, that marked the start of the preparation of the first Passover Festival of Unleavened Bread meal. He was deposed from the cross and entombed later that very Friday afternoon. The basis for this conclusion is that all four gospels agree that Jesus's body was deposed from the cross supposedly due to the stigma of crucifixion victims being left hanging on a preparation day, whose sacred meal, by command, would be eaten at the coming sunset, a sunset that happened also to commence a Sabbath. Hence, since the Sabbath is not a moveable day and is always a Saturday, that particular preparation day must have been a Friday, in fact 15 Nisan, the imminent day, 16 Nisan, a Sabbath (Matthew 27:12–25, Mark 15:42–44, Luke 23:54, John 19:31) being a Saturday.

Even so, there has existed a disinclination to allow a concurrence of all four gospels as to the day and date of the execution itself, as distinct from that of Jesus's verified death. The disinclination seems to be rooted in four locutions, three of which are found in the fourth gospel, and the fourth due to Paul. The fourth will be discussed separately from the other three.

Of the three, one relates to the fear of ritual impurity or contamination when the chief priests and scribes delivered Jesus to Pilate, were they to enter the Gentile Roman premises before they could eat their Passover meal. As John 18:28 (NRSV) states it: "Then they took Jesus from Caiaphas to Pilate's headquarters. It was early in the morning. They themselves did not enter the headquarters so as to avoid ritual defilement and to be able to eat the Passover." A second identifies the day in question as the day of preparation, but not of which Passover. John 19:14 (NRSV) states: "Now, it was the day of Preparation for the Passover; and it was about noon. He said to the Jews, 'Here is your King!'" The third relates to Jesus's sentiments before the Passover festival. John 13:1–2 (NRSV) states: "Now, before the festival of the Passover, Jesus knew that his hour had come to depart this world and go to the Father. Having loved his own who were in the world, he loved them to the end. The devil had already put it into the heart of Judas son of Simon Iscariot to betray him." Many readers surmise from those passages that the references to Passover were references to the Passover of the Lamb, rather than the Passover Feast of Unleavened Bread, and infer from that surmise that the supper that Jesus had earlier been in the course of eating had not been a Passover of the Lamb meal, and indeed that by the commencement of the actual Passover of the Lamb meal, Jesus was already crucified, dead, and buried.

With regard to the fear of contamination, the chief priests and scribes who delivered Jesus to Pilate were well-advised to avoid Pilate's Gentile premises, where there should be every expectation of the presence of leavening. Were the priests to enter those premises, they would no longer be able to present themselves as thoroughly deleavened, a rigid prerequisite for celebrating Passover. If that day were to be the day of preparation of the Passover lamb, those chief priests and scribes should indeed be precluded from eating that sacred meal later in the evening, and it would be too late for them now to try and certifiably deleaven themselves again for that meal. They would, however, not be excused from observing Passover altogether (e.g., Numbers 9:10–11), but would be consigned to a makeup Passover later, on the same date of the following month).

As already shown, two Passover celebrations were prescribed, the longer Passover of Unleavened Bread following on the heels of the one-day Passover of the Lamb. Both observances were Paschal, and were so designated in Tanakh and the New Testament and Josephus. When Josephus was writing toward the close of the century, at about the same time as John was finishing his gospel, the Feast of Unleavened Bread was still known as Passover. By then, however, the celebration of the Passover of the Lamb had been completely discontinued by reason of the destruction of the temple. Josephus, in Jewish Antiquities, specifically states "the Jews were celebrating the Feast of Unleavened Bread, which we call the Passover" (18.2.2).

Even though it is common to think of the Passover of the Lamb at the mention of Passover, in Israel today Passover is observed exclusively as the Festival of Unleavened Bread. Since the Passover of the Lamb and the Feast of Unleavened Bread were both known as Passover during the entire New Testament period, it becomes necessary to determine which of the *two* Passovers it was whose "preparation day" caused the chief priests and scribes to recoil from entering Pilate's premises. To do so, it is necessary to take a look at the three references to the "day of preparation" in John, all of which occur in chapter 19 at verses 14, 31, and 42.

John 19:31 (NRSV) is the fulcrum. It states: "Since it was the day of Preparation, the Jews did not want the bodies left on the cross during the Sabbath, especially because that Sabbath was a day of great solemnity. So they asked Pilate to have the legs of the crucified men broken and the bodies removed."

It should be noted that two reasons are not being offered Pilate, one relating to the preparation day and the other to the Sabbath. Indeed, if a body should not be hanging on a preparation day, then it would be illogical to be seeking a crucifixion on a preparation day in John's gospel, and on the day of preparation of the Passover of the Lamb meal in the Synoptic Gospels. Rather, the reason surely relates to the propinquity of that solemn Sabbath. This particular reference to a preparation day relates to a request made of Pontius Pilate in the afternoon of a preparation day. If it refers to the preparation of the Passover lamb, and so was made on the Thursday afternoon, after the crucifixion had already taken place, what reason could there have been to worry about bodies hanging on the cross into the Sabbath day, which would still be more than twenty-four hours away? After all, by the time the Sabbath arrived, the victim might well be dead, and the whole matter moot.

On the contrary, the urgency of the request to Pilate undoubtedly reflected the *imminence* of that particular solemn Sabbath, and so would seem to indicate that the request was made on the afternoon of 15 Nisan, a few hours before sunset and the onset of that Sabbath. Since the crucifixion and the request would in this case have occurred on the same day (John 19:30–31), and in light of Pilate's surprise that Jesus could have died already, that day clearly had to have been the Friday. The indicated special solemnity of that approaching particular Sabbath would then make the timely deposition of the crucified bodies seem a matter of urgent necessity.

A similar impression is gained when the references in Mark and Luke are juxtaposed with the reference in John. It is instructive to note the references to the preparation day in the two Synoptic Gospels, Mark and Luke. Each refers to Friday, and neither of them to Thursday. Mark 15:42 (NRSV): "And when evening was come, because it was the preparation and that was the day before the Sabbath ..." Luke 23:54 (NRSV): "And it was the day of the preparation and the Sabbath was drawing near." Now, juxtapose the reference in John's gospel (19:31 NRSV): "Since it was the day of Preparation, the Jews did not want the bodies left on the cross during the Sabbath, especially because that Sabbath was a day of great solemnity. So they asked Pilate to have the legs of the crucified men broken and the bodies removed." It would seem that all three citations refer to the same day, Friday, and all three connect the preparation day to that Sabbath, not the Thursday.

It is commonly thought that it was the mere threat of bodies left hanging into a Sabbath, which would have been scandalous. As a matter of fact, there would have been no qualms about a body being left hanging, or even being handled on a Sabbath day, except when ritual purity would be compromised and so prevent some necessary function.

Josephus (Jewish Antiquities 18.2.2) relates an incident in which certain obnoxious Samaritans sneaked into Jerusalem and scattered corpses in the temple cloisters. This occurred when the gates were opened, as was the custom, soon after midnight after the eating of the supper of the first day of the Feast of Unleavened Bread, and so several hours into the Sabbath. That Sabbath was, like 16 Nisan, AD 33, a Passover Sabbath, a solemn or High Sabbath. Its solemnity did not prevent, in that particular grave case, the prompt evacuation of the corpses. Samaritans were forthwith barred from the temple, even from festivals to which they had in the past been admitted, and the temple guards thenceforth watched the grounds more studiously.

What would have made the burial of Jesus urgent was not so much the fact of an impending Sabbath as the requirement, under Judaic law and custom, of a same-day burial as the occurrence of death whenever possible. Deuteronomy 21:22–23 (NRSV), lays it down that "when someone is convicted of a crime punishable by death and is executed, and you hang him on a tree, his corpse must not remain all night upon the tree; you shall bury him that same day, for anyone hung on a tree is under God's curse. You must not defile the land that the Lord your God is giving you for possession." In fact, since Jesus was a Jew accused of a capital crime by the Sanhedrin and condemned to death, the high priest himself, and certainly Jesus's own blood relatives, were under obligation to do everything possible to ensure that he would receive a same-day burial, or at least a next-day one, even when that day would be an ordinary Sabbath.

Because, however, the impending Sabbath in Jesus's case was a solemn High Sabbath, ordinary burial rites on that High Sabbath day would be entirely out of the question. There was thus no alternative to the initiation of Jesus's burial on that Friday, even if the completion had to be deferred till the day after that High

Sabbath. That was why the three Marys had to suspend Jesus's burial rites midway and wait till the end of the Passover Sabbath in order to complete them. On this occasion, it fell on Joseph of Arimathea, a probable relative of Jesus, to see to the retrieval of Jesus's body and to ensure his same-day burial before the beginning of that High Sabbath.

What is it that makes a Passover Sabbath, like the one in John's gospel, great, high, or solemn? It is nothing other than the fact that such a Passover Sabbath is the occasion when the Jewish liturgical calendar is set, including fixing the dates of the Feast of First Fruits and of Pentecost. In general, no work unconnected with the liturgical calendar could take place on a High Sabbath, even work that might normally be done on a regular Sabbath. In the case of the High Sabbath, such work is brought forward to the preceding Friday. That is why the Friday immediately preceding a High Sabbath became known as *preparation day,* a day for performing all needed work that must not be done on the High Sabbath day itself on account of its great solemnity. Such a day was Friday, 15 Nisan, in AD 33. It is clear now that that Friday's being a preparation day had nothing at all to do with the preparation of the Passover of the Lamb meal, which was already over, or the first meal of the Feast of Unleavened Bread, both of which were in fact simply prepared on normal schedule.

Would Jesus have been tried on that Friday, the first day of the Feast of Unleavened Bread, and also the day before a High Sabbath? Without a doubt! Even though a law dating back to Deuteronomy (NRSV) forbade the convening of a court on a feast day, certain offenses were exempted. Among the exempted offenses were contumacious disobedience toward a priest who went into the Holy of Holies. All of the exceptions were naturally grave and were punishable by death (17:12–13), generally exacted by mass stoning, followed at times by hanging on a tree (21–22).

Delay in trying such capital offenses, such as Jesus was in the end charged with, or in carrying out the capital sentence it called for, only compounded the original offense. The execution was required to be public, as Jesus's was, in order to instill the fear of Almighty God. Apparently, less than four decades earlier than Jesus's own case, Jeshu, a disciple of Rabbi Joshua Ben Perachia, had been condemned on charges of being a sorcery-mongering apostate, and was hanged by order of the Sanhedrin on Passover (cf Babylonian Talmud, Sanhedrin 43a).

Even though Caiaphas had originally only designated Jesus a ransom sacrifice for Judea, the Sanhedrin were forced to pin capital charges on him in order to justify his execution. Caiaphas's particular capital charges were among those exempted from the proscription regarding holding court on feast days. Jesus would have been given a rapid trial, condemned, and executed without delay if only the Sanhedrin had had capital authority at that time. Jesus would have been executed by mass stoning, and his body would then have been hanged. Next, his body would have been left hanging for the rest of the day, until it was finally removed from the tree. Since Jesus was a Jew, he would have had to be given a same-day burial, albeit an "obscure" and "ignominous" one, because such a person would have been deemed to be accursed of God. As it was, Jesus did receive a rapid trial and condemnation at the hands of Caiaphas's Sanhedrin. The execution, however, would only be by leave of Pontius Pilate, and so could not be as rapid as Jesus's case demanded.

It should be noted that the execution of Jesus would itself produce a corpse, whether on the day of the Passover of the Lamb (14 Nisan) or on the commencement day of the Feast of Unleavened Bread (15 Nisan). It was only because Jesus's was a Roman execution that it became necessary to seek permission from Pilate in order to depose his body for Jewish burial. But for Jesus's expiration, however, there would have been nothing execrable about his body continuing to hang on the cross on account of his being a Roman execution. The other two victims, who were still alive, presumably did continue to hang on their crosses into the Sabbath. Since, however, Jesus had already died and, especially, being a Jew accused of blasphemy, he required a same-day burial (Deuteronomy 21:22), and the imminence of the Passover Sabbath made his burial preparation a rushed, and apparently incomplete, affair. For the same cause, he had to be entombed in a nearby sepulcher (19:42), one providentially offered by Joseph of Arimathea.

As a matter of fact, the bodies of victims of Roman crucifixion were typically left hanging for days to decompose on their crosses even in Judea. The reason this did not happen in Jesus's case, even though the execution was Roman, was that Pilate had initially doubted his guilt. He had found no fault in Jesus, who seemed to him from reports to have even seemed favorably disposed toward the Romans. Moreover, Pilate was in all probability still smarting over the fact that his hands had been forced with the threat of an unfavorable report to the emperor about his reluctance to move against a manifest enemy of Rome who had encouraged crowds to call him king of the Jews. Besides, Pilate stood to gain satisfaction from doing Jesus a final favor and from paying back the Sanhedrin and the people, both by refusing to amend his titulus, which described Jesus as the king of the Jews, and by having Jesus's body released untypically early to Joseph of Arimathea, a Jesus partisan, subject only to his actual death being verified (Psalm 16:10, 49:9; Acts 3:31, 37).

It has so far been shown that the entire calendric question flows from a misunderstanding of the phrase "preparation day." The early church and Saint Augustine clearly understood the expression "preparation day" to relate to a solemn Sabbath, and that is why the early church and Saint Augustine could find no calendric question in their reading of the four gospels.

In none of the Gospels would Jesus live to observe the seven-day Festival of Unleavened Bread. It is to be noted that the fourth gospel here in fact refers to the Passover festival or feast (tes heortes), a designation that the Gospels apply to the Feast of Unleavened Bread but not to the meal of the Passover lamb. It is to this feast and not to the meal of the lamb that John refers (John 13:1–2), for in the context of what Jesus was engaged in at that point, the Festival of Unleavened Bread would actually be insignificant. It would not be eaten by Jesus. The Passover meal of the lamb would, on the other hand, be fraught with analogical meaning.

When Judas abruptly left the table, some of the disciples mistakenly thought Jesus had asked him to go out and buy what would be needed for the Feast of Unleavened Bread (John 13:29), not for the Passover of the Lamb meal, which was not called a feast, and which they were at that time in the course of eating. The disciples had in mind the Feast of Unleavened Bread, which was very much imminent at that point. There should be little doubt that the meal from which Judas exited early was the Passover of the Lamb meal. It should also be evident that at the time when Jesus and his disciples were at their supper, it was that meal which was being eaten by every other Jew in Jerusalem. What should we imagine to have been their own fare when Jesus and his disciples supped on the same night?

It was right after eating the Passover lamb that Jesus celebrated the Mass of the Last Supper. This juxtaposition signified the supplanting of one by the other. Just as the Passover of the Lamb symbolized the passage of the Israelites from their enslavement to Pharaoh to the freedom of the people of God, so the body and blood of Christ became to Paul the symbol of our passage from the enslavement of sin to the liberty of the people of God. Paul was inspired by this similitude of case to declare that Christ has been sacrificed as our Passover, and become our own Paschal lamb (1 Corinthians 5:7), referring to the body and blood of Christ consumed at the Last Supper and at every eucharistic meal.

This statement of Paul's is sometimes taken to show that Jesus was slain on the Thursday afternoon before the Passover meal just like a Passover lamb, thereby pushing Jesus's Last Supper into the previous (Wednesday) night. But in this way, there would be no synchronicity between the consumption of Jesus's last supper and Eucharist and the eating of the Passover lamb! Besides, this would also make Jesus's body hang on the cross all through the eating of the actual sacred Passover lamb meal, and well into the first day of the Feast of Unleavened Bread, this even though he was supposed to have died after only a few hours.

Furthermore, as regards Paul's assimilation, his analogy could not have envisaged Jesus's execution at all, since the Passover lamb of the Israelites was never an atonement sacrifice, unlike Jesus's execution. The Passover lamb was not even the means of the liberation of the Israelites from Egyptian bondage, but only its marker, whereas the body and blood of Christ have a full-fledged redemptive function, as Paul in particular very well knew.

What Jesus's approaching departure would leave him no time for was the Passover Festival (13:1) and not the Passover lamb meal. For the latter, his timing had been perfect. It being now the early hours of the day after the Passover of the Lamb, the day of the Festival of Unleavened Bread had just begun. The period of preparation for its first meal would only begin later in the afternoon that day, Friday, 15 Nisan, and its meat dishes and unleavened bread would have to be readied by evening, twilight, or sunset, with the feasting itself only commencing thereafter, during the opening hours of Saturday, 16 Nisan, a Sabbath. Jesus knew that he would not be around for that High Sabbath to celebrate that festival, for his hour of departure was already at hand, and his Passion would begin not long after his current supper. While all ordinary work was indeed forbidden on the two days, 14 and 15 Nisan, as well as on the final day of the weeklong festival, the chief priests and scribes would unawares be busy at no ordinary work but the world's salvation.

An attempt is frequently made to cast doubt on the chronology with the claim that while the date of each Passover is fixed, its day of the week is variable. It is claimed that we are therefore not able to determine on which day of the week Passover fell in which year. Christians talking only to other Christians may well experience some befuddlement in sorting out the days of the week on which Passover falls. On matters such as this, however, it would surely be better for Christians to consult Jewish authorities. It is very much to be doubted whether the chief rabbinate experiences any such befuddlement. Without doubt, it is completely clear to them on which day of the week each Passover would fall in any given year. It would be of the same order of piquancy were people of other than a Christian faith to say that because the day of the week of Easter is fixed while its date is variable, we are not able to determine on which date Easter falls in which year.

In the present case, however, even Christians have no excuse to be confused, since all four gospels now make it clear that that particular Passover of the Lamb was on a Thursday, and that it flowed into a "preparation day," which was the eve of a High Sabbath, and so a Friday. It is advisedly that this entire section is based on *Jewish* discussions.

The question must still be addressed why, in his gospel account, John underplayed the Passover of the Lamb. It should be remarked that by the time John settled down to finishing the fourth gospel, the Jerusalem temple had been lying in ruins for upwards of two decades. Jesus had in fact foretold that particular calamity (Matthew 24:2, Mark 13:2, Luke 21:6). The utter destruction of the temple made it impossible to carry out any of those worshipful acts centered on the temple. Among them was the Passover of the Lamb. In fact, that particular act of devotion totally ceased, though it remained possible to celebrate the Passover of Unleavened Bread. By the middle of the final decade of the first century AD, when John finished his gospel, it had been crystal clear to him that, at Jesus's final supper with his disciples, the Passover of the Lamb was already a moribund observance. It could therefore not have played any role at all, let alone a significant one, except analogically, in the forward-looking momentous observances that Jesus was promulgating.

Therein, however, lay a conundrum. By command, the Passover, which is today celebrated only as the Feast of Unleavened Bread, was to be observed throughout the generations of the Israelites. Also by demand of the Law, the setting of the slaughtering of the lamb, as well as the collection of its fat and kidneys, was to be on the temple grounds: Deuteronomy 16:5 (NRSV): "You are not permitted to offer the passover sacrifice within any of your towns that the LORD your God is giving you. But at the place that the LORD your God will choose as a dwelling for his name."

As to any idea of its cessation, Jesus had said that the law would be fulfilled down to its last jot and iota, even while also foretelling the temple's complete destruction. The composers of the Synoptic Gospels, who surely wrote somewhat before this calamity, did not quite appreciate the seeming tension. Because John wrote only after the destruction of the temple, he himself could not have been oblivious to it. As to Paul, who claimed to have been directly inspired by Jesus himself, he felt it all too keenly, as evidenced by his tortuous grappling with the question of the very origin and validity of the law.

It should simply have followed from Jesus's remarks that the Law's fulfillment would have to have been achieved by the time of the temple's destruction. Also, since Jesus announced that he himself had come to fulfill the Law, it likewise should have followed that Jesus had to fulfill the Law in his own lifetime. It would be in Jesus's life that the Law would be fulfilled, in other words, observed and never contravened, for the first and only time in history.

The original Passover of the Lamb related to God's deliverance of his people from slavery and oppression under Pharaoh. Retrospectively, it would be clearer still to John that the Passover of the Lamb, which was celebrated during Jesus's final night with his apostles, marked the completion of the existing dispensation, which would already have been in the process of being supplanted by a new and larger worldwide deliverance with its own new dispensation. It was bound to be supplanted sooner or later in any case with the installation of the expected Messiah, whenever that was agreed to be, for that would bring the longed for and permanent deliverance, and represent a new and final Passover.

For Christians, too, the old Passover of the Lamb is replaced by a new and final Passover of the Lamb of God. This time, it would not be the firstborn of the Romans who would die, but the only Son of God, and the new deliverance would be not from any earthly power but from unseen forces of evil, sin, and death.

Once the Israelites were no longer subject to Pharaoh's laws, they needed the Mosaic law to regulate their relation to God, their relations to one another, and their relations to the widow and stranger among them. In the case of the new redemption from the slavery of sin, however, the relations would be totally marked by the love of God, the universal practice of love and of doing unto others as we would have them do unto us.

The life and death of Jesus himself for the first time fully satisfied the demands of the law of love—even to the extent of taking over our sins and dying in our place, thereby "cancelling the record of debt that stood against us with its legal demands, setting it aside by nailing it to the cross" (Colossians 2:14). "Christ is the end of the Law unto righteousness to everyone that believes" (Romans 10:4). Christ's new injunction demands not sentimental love, which cannot be enjoined, but practical love, which can; it does not urge that we be in love with our neighbor, only that we show our neighbor love. Paul taught the Galatians that the whole law is fulfilled in one statement, namely, "you shall love your neighbor as yourself" (Galatians 5:14).

The new act by which Jesus was to free us from slavery to sin and its oppression was his own crucifixion and resurrection. When the Israelites were themselves freed from slavery to Pharaoh, they became distinguished by a continuing male circumcision and a set of codes detailing their responsibility to God and their responsibility to one another. With the impending freedom from the bondage of sin, we were all now to be characterized by a universal baptism in the name of the Father, and of the Son and of the Holy Spirit, and by adherence to a new way of detailing our responsibility to God and to one another. Our responsibility to God remains the same and requires us to love him with all our heart, and all our soul, and our entire mind, and all our strength. It speaks to our bond as one and all children of God. We owe our love to God, and so, in our responsibility to one another, we come also to owe it without exception to everyone who has been fashioned in the image of God.

It was because the authors of the Synoptic Gospels hewed to the then current Halakhah view of the Law that they did not particularly emphasize Jesus's new injunction, which was actually founded in Torah. Just as the meal of the Passover lamb enshrined the liberation from Pharaoh, so now the eating of the flesh and drinking of the blood of the Lamb of God enshrine our new liberation from sin. By contrast, though, consuming the body and blood of Christ becomes not merely the symbol but recalls the very means of the new deliverance.

John had no need to emphasize the Passover of the Lamb, since its observance had long ceased by the time he was actually writing his gospel. The new emphasis was now to be on the milieu promulgated by Jesus Christ.

CHAPTER 10

JESUS AND PAUL ON THE NATURE OF THE LAW

It ought to be considered that when Jesus spoke cherishingly of the law, he did not quite mean the totality of Judaic law, or Halakhah, which comprised the 613 mitzvot, or commandments of Torah amplified by an indefinite number of equally binding mitzvot d'rabbanan, those added by rabbis. It is equally clear that when Paul spoke of the Law, he could only have meant this composite Judaic law, in which he was indeed very well versed above his peers. However, it is not this Judaic law, or Halakhah, that Jesus said he had come to fulfill, for Jesus often deprecated some of its mandates, caustically decrying them as setting aside God's own commandments in favor of the traditions of men (Mark 7:7–13). In this, Jesus was clearly contrasting Judaic law with the law of God, not identifying them with each other. Indeed, on quite a few occasions, he publicly contravened some of those binding mandates in favor of the demands of compassion and love, which are always required by the law of God. Besides, Jesus was fully aware that, with the coming destruction of the temple, the entire integrity of the Judaic law would be badly fractured, but never the law of God, which has no ending. Malachi 2:6 (TNIV), in a passage that applies to Jesus, says of him that "true instruction was in his mouth, and nothing false was found on his lips!"

Tanakh itself fully grasped the true law as Jesus understood and proclaimed it. That law was dual, comprising the law of love in relation to God and the law of love in relation to all others. It was that dual command, rather than the numerous mandates and ordinances, which was the true law declared by Jesus to be the whole Law and the Prophets. It was this dual law that Jesus said he had come to fulfill not annul and that he had said would endure until heaven and earth passed away (Matthew 5:17–18). The leaders of the Jerusalem church, on the other hand, identified the law with the Judaic law and regarded that law as the key to righteousness before God. Hence they understood Jesus's proclamation of the validity and permanence of the law to be the validity and permanence of the entire Judaic law, which they themselves had fully held to be divine in both origin and authority. It is clear that such was not the evangelist John's own belief during the time that he was completing his gospel, nor even earlier on, on the evidence of his letters, in which the law he constantly preached was that of love.

In hewing to the permanence of the Judaic law, the Jerusalem church only saw Jesus as the fulfillment of messianic prophecy, and so as being fully embedded in the Law and the Prophets. They would not see him as someone who came to promulgate what would have seemed to them an alternative route to righteousness before God. To be sure, the Jerusalem church saw themselves as pitted in a doctrinal struggle with Pharisees, priests, and scribes regarding the theological significance of the life, death, and especially resurrection of Jesus. For the Jerusalem church, the Judaic law, around which Judaic doctrine and practice were built, incontrovertibly stood valid. Did the apostles not have Jesus's own pronouncement regarding the validity and durability of the law to support them? Accordingly, all who wished to accept fellowship with them as followers of Jesus Christ should already be Jews immersed in the fullness of Judaic law, or be proselytes to Judaism, who would then only need to accept Jesus as Judaism's prophesied Messiah. All their males would as a matter of course require to be circumcised.

Indeed, even Peter, who had been directly instructed in visions to induct Gentiles such as the unproselytized centurion Cornelius, was at the same time apologetic, saying (Acts 10:28 NRSV), "You yourselves know that it is unlawful for a Jew to associate with or visit with a Gentile; but God has shown me that I should not call anyone profane or unclean."

For Paul, on the other hand, as also for the apostle John, a gulf did exist between that Judaic law and the new Christianity. Following his illumination on his way to Damascus, Paul came to fully accept faith in Jesus Christ as the only path to righteousness, a revelation that sharply conflicted with the Judaic belief in the redeeming power of Judaic law. Paul reasoned that if Jesus was really the Way, Judaic law could not concurrently be a God-sanctioned regimen for righteousness before him, as distinct from righteousness before men. And so, in spite of his own rigorous training at the feet of Gamaliel, he flirted for a while with the extreme idea that the Judaic law, together with the salvific claim made on its behalf, must have been delivered at the behest of an angel, and an ill-disposed one at that. The difficulty in this for Paul was that Jesus himself had pronounced positively on the validity and authority of the law, as the Jerusalem leaders no doubt hastened to instruct him, especially during his dispute with them during the Jerusalem Council. The Law absolutely could not be nullified, even if certain aspects could be relaxed in order to accommodate Gentiles, who would never become children of Abraham anyhow, not having had Abraham for an ancestor!

Since, following his conversion, Paul came to hold that it was faith in Jesus Christ, rather than scrupulous adherence to Judaic law, which was the avenue to righteousness, it quickly became evident to him that either the Judaic law could not have been God-given and so had no permanent validity, or else it was God-given but was intended not as an avenue to righteousness but to a different end. He championed first the one but in the end the other hypothesis. It was under the first hypothesis that Paul thought Judaic law must have originally been delivered at the behest of an angel as an incubus on the people. His idea was that it was the existence of the law that created the possibility of sin, every breach of it becoming a sin. Under the second hypothesis, which was his final view, the Judaic law did indeed have a divine origin, but its purpose was not to lead us to righteousness but to teach us obedience until the arrival of Jesus Christ, who would disclose to us the true path to righteousness before God.

Paul's view that the Judaic law had little to do with righteousness before God actually consorted well with Jesus's own declaration during one of his confrontations with scribes and Pharisees. Widely noted as inveterate sticklers after the law, who did their utmost to observe it in all its particulars, they felt able to assure Jesus that they themselves were without sin. In response, Jesus told them that that conviction only mired them in their sin. Notable also is Jesus's story about the two men who went to pray. One had always followed Judaic law and evidently considered himself righteous before God. The other, who could make no such claim for himself, threw himself instead on the mercy of God. The latter, but not the former, became justified before God. In his own preaching, John the Baptist exhorted his hearers to repentance rather than to even more fastidious adherence to Judaic law. Scrupulousness with respect to Judaic law did not confer righteousness before God or bring one to salvation, for, before God, there still would be no one perfect. He, the Baptist, would usher in an end, not to the law of God, but to Judaic law and to prophecy as well; for, close on his heels, was to appear the Lamb of God, the fulfiller of prophecy, who would truly take away sins, and expound anew the real way to righteousness and to God.

Paul was the one who seemed to find some way to unravel the conundrum. To Paul in his new view, the law, understood always by him as Judaic law, now only exacted obedience, and in fact convicted us of the sin of disobedience with each lapse on our part. No one became perfect by observing the law (Hebrews 7:19), nor attained righteousness by such means (Galatians 3:11). The Mosaic law, the kernel of Judaic law, commanded obedience, and the Deuteronomic promise to those who obeyed it, its adherents and observers, was always long life, prosperity, and possession in the Promised Land, never justification or salvation from death. Even so, Judaic belief steadfastly held on to the sufficiency of Judaic law, which was an expansion of the Mosaic law, for personal righteousness or justification before God. It allowed for no other way.

Consequently, adherents and practitioners of Judaic law strenuously opposed those followers of Jesus who, well after his resurrection and ascension, started preaching their own way derived from Jesus's teachings as the true Way of Salvation. It was to be this new way alone that would be capable of conferring righteousness, and of leading to justification before God, and hence to salvation from permanent death.

Indeed, it was solely to distinguish between the two camps that the evangelist John, writing long after the event, came to refer to the sticklers after the Judaic law as "the Jews." That law did teach *obedience* to God, but the new way taught *trust* in God. Even so, it does stand that without obedience there can be no trust. Thus it was that Paul came to hold, concerning the Judaic law, that it "is holy, and the commandment is holy and just and good" (Romans

7:12 NRSV), and indeed to be upheld, for that law was our tutor until Christ came, so that we can now be justified, but by faith.

How may this be understood? There is at bottom only one law in fact, separating out as love of God and love of neighbor. That indeed was the law reached for in the Ten Commandments, which express in sample detail our love of God and our love of our neighbor. Both Tanakh and Jesus agree that that is the heart of the Law. Accordingly, it is the love of God and the love of our neighbor, which are the two demands of Jesus's own formulation. Jesus's formulation was not a new command, but a new injunction (ἡ ἐντολὴ) as to how the law of God was to inform our lives and be fulfilled: to love God, and to love one another as Jesus had loved his disciples. In this connection, our conscience becomes a manifestation of lapses in our love.

What, then, is the dispute between the Jerusalem church and Paul and his followers?

Although Tanakh fully recognized the combined law of love, its method of implementing the combined law was to initiate hundreds of individual precepts to cover individual types of situations of which advance cognizance would be taken. It is clear that in this enumerative way it would be impossible to anticipate every type of situation to which the combined law should in fact apply. Those specific precepts, be they ever so many, simply cannot be exhaustive of all possible such situations. And, for both the Jerusalem church and earlier for Paul himself, the Law was precisely the enumerative Judaic law.

This enumerative approach alone must guarantee that human conduct would be replete with errors, defaults, and contraventions of the combined law of love. This enumerative method of Judaic law was bound to guarantee sinfulness, for as Paul clearly saw, its enumerations could not possibly ever spell out in complete detail and in advance every situation in which the Law itself should apply. Any detailed spelling out of the law would in virtue of its inescapable incompleteness guarantee sinning.

If Paul had personally heard Jesus, he would have realized from the start that, to Jesus, the Law was not the enumerative Judaic law but the dual law of love. After Paul came to the conclusion that Torah law together with its rabbinical amplifications was only meant to teach obedience and not righteousness, he also came to grasp that the true Law was wholly a law of love, just as Jesus had taught without his first-hand knowledge. Now he himself started extolling the law of love. Practice of the law in this dual form would secure righteousness before God, for in it lies holiness. In preaching faith through Jesus Christ, Paul also said that in Christ Jesus the only thing that availed was faith that worked through love (Galatians 5:6). And at Romans 13:10, he roundly declared that love was the fulfilling of the Law. Paul had come to realize that it was actually the law as the dual law of love that Jesus had said could not be abrogated, expire, or fall into abeyance, even if the temple were to be destroyed. As to Judaic law itself, it should, like prophecy, have begun to reach a crisis with the arrival of John the Baptist, who taught the habit of repentance and conversion in preparation for the one who would imminently baptize in the Holy Spirit and fire (Matthew 3:11) and teach the unflagging practice of love.

Is there an alternative way, besides the mandates of Judaic law, to fulfill the combined law of love? Any alternative way will have to abandon anticipatory rules and precepts in order to avoid the creation of sin; in other words, abandon the letter of the law (mandates), and instead heartily embrace its spirit (love). This will often cause us to act in ways that would be at variance with the letter of the Halakhah enumeration, even while promoting its spirit. This means that in our relations with God, we at all times and in every circumstance show him our love with all our heart and all our soul and all our mind and all our strength, and in every relation with our neighbor we act exclusively from a loving disposition. To the extent that we do this, we will not be sinning, and if we always do this, we will be holy as our Father is holy. It is precisely this that led Jesus to heal the sick on a Sabbath day. Indeed, this is how Jesus fulfilled the law in his own earthly life, by constantly and in all things acting out of love toward his Father and out of love toward mankind. And this is how he taught us to fulfill the law in the statement of his total formulation of the law, his dual so-called commandment or injunction, whose newness consisted simply in its replacing the mandates of the Judaic law.

To the extent that we have reduced the combined law of love to a host of statutes, codes, decrees, rules, and precepts, we have all inevitably departed from the combined law, which does not dwell in such things but only in loving actions and deeds of love.

Since enumerative law makes sinners of us all, it creates a need for our redemption from the consequence of our sin. The inability of the enumerative law to confer righteousness is its real shortcoming, despite all the sacrifices performed over centuries the world over. Jeremiah deprecatingly made the utterance: "I did not speak to them or command them concerning burnt offerings and sacrifices" (Jeremiah 7:22 NRSV). On the other hand, Paul, now in full realization, proclaimed that the commandments are summed up in this word: "'Love your neighbor as yourself.' … therefore, love is the fulfilling of the law." (Romans 13:8–10 NRSV).

The Sadducees, who did not believe in a resurrection from the dead, properly appreciated this nonsalvific limitation of the Judaic law, even while also following its precepts as a guide to life on earth. On the other hand, in coming to do God's will, not only did Jesus fulfill the law of love, he also completed the Judaic law by supplying what was lacking in it, namely a means of attaining (or being credited with) righteousness or justification before God, for Jew and Gentile alike, and hence the prospect of salvation from death; in other words, everlasting life. When God's will is done on earth as it is in heaven, the earth becomes an extension of heaven itself.

Practitioners of the law by schedule honored God through their obedience; but it is through a faith-inspired practice of love that one can be justified before God, and so obtain peace with him (Romans 5:1–2). Faith that expresses itself through works of love of God and works of love of neighbor completely bypasses our failures with the schedules of the enumerative law.

The debt of our sins has been appropriated by Jesus, who arranged to settle it for us on the cross of Golgotha. We cannot rely wholly on our own inner resources in the endeavor to live our lives entirely in the spirit of the combined law of love; for this, we need trust in Jesus Christ and his grace. That is our only way to righteousness and salvation (Galatians 2:16).

Paul brilliantly illustrated much of this in his discussion of the case of the patriarch Abraham. Abraham's obedience to God in uprooting himself from Ur of the Chaldeans only earned him, as with the later Deuteronomic promise, the promise of land and prosperity for himself and his descendants. However, it was not for this astonishing act of obedience that he earned the sobriquet of righteousness. He earned that only by proving his trust in God when he attempted to sacrifice his only son, Isaac, at God's behest, even while being mindful of God's earlier promise that it would be through that very same Isaac that Abraham would eventually have a descendant in whom all the nations of the earth would be blessed. It was only for this stunning trustfulness against all reason that he was pronounced *righteous*—and friend of God—all this ahead of the Ten Commandments and their Halakhah expansion!

Paul's analysis of the case of Abraham confirmed this to him. According to God's covenant with Abraham, justification and righteousness in general would come not through his descendants as a whole, his seeds, but only through a single descendant (Galatians 3:16), the one seed who was destined to be the harbinger of the salvation that God had prepared in the sight of every people, a light to reveal God to all nations and to be the glory of God's people Israel, according to the words of Simeon's Canticle. This was indeed the very point of the genealogy in Matthew 1:1–16 and in Luke 3:23–38. The glory of Israel would not lie in being Abraham's biological descendants at large, even though to the descendants at large indeed belong the patriarchs, and to their race belongs the Christ according to the flesh (Romans 9:4).

That genealogy was meant to delineate the sequence of God's reiterations of Abraham's blessing. Beginning with Abraham himself, the line passed through Isaac, but not Ishmael, through Jacob, but not Esau, and so on through Obed, Jesse, and David, each time bypassing all their brothers and sisters, and continuing similarly until it ended with the annunciation. It is noteworthy that the angel that appeared in a vision to Joseph, descendant of David through Solomon in Matthew and Nathan in Luke, did not reiterate that blessing to him, but encouraged him instead to keep Mary, his betrothed, whom the angel identified as the mother of the one who would save his people from their sins and be a blessing to all nations, and thus the long awaited seed of Abraham.

If the truth be told, and the male bias of Judaic genealogy be set aside, it was to the Virgin Mary, female descendant of Abraham and

David, that the final iteration was addressed, when the archangel Gabriel announced to Mary her prospective motherhood, as the time arrived for the long-promised descendant to be born. The male bias of the genealogy traced the promise through Solomon (Matthew) or Nathan (Luke), two of the three sons of David by Bathsheba, and ancestor of Joseph, husband of Mary. In fact, the promise seems to have been carried not through Solomon but through Nathan, a son of David, to whom Mary owed her own ancestry, according to the conjecture of John of Damascus, which Bonaventure also endorsed. Micah's prophecy (Micah 5:1–3), Matthew 1:18–23, the archangel Gabriel's annunciation, and the dream angel's reassurance to Joseph, when taken together, surely grant to Mary—a virgin by implication of the oneiric declaration to Joseph—the exclusive claim to being the recipient of the final iteration. Jesus put a twist on this himself when he suggested that Abraham had rejoiced to see his day, and was, like David, only paradoxically alluded to as his ancestor. In fact, there exists no patrilineal descent to Jesus from Abraham or from David.

Jesus was the fulfiller of the promise of that unilineal reiteration. He and he alone was the particular seed of Abraham (through Mary) in whom all the nations of the earth would be blessed. The same thing was revealed to the prophet Isaiah when he said, "A bruised reed he will not break, a smoldering wick he will not quench, until he brings justice to victory; in his name, the gentiles will hope." This is also the recognition of Simeon in his canticle, "Nunc dimittis," when, upon beholding the infant Jesus, he proclaimed him to be a light unto the nations and the glory of God's people Israel (Luke 2:29–32). And this became Paul's own eventual understanding (Galatians 3:16). The light of revelation to the nations, in which we should all be blessed, was never going to be the plenitude of Abraham's biological descendants. It was always going to be specific to the infant Jesus alone, by whom the blessing would be consummated.

A parallel narrowing singled out Judah out of the Twelve Tribes, and, from the cities and towns of Judah, singled out Bethlehem, from which the Chosen One would hail. "And you, oh Bethlehem, in the land of Judah, from you shall come a ruler who shall shepherd my people" (Matthew 2:6; also Micah 5:1–3).

Through such analysis, Paul established the prior claim of trust in God over fidelity to Judaic law, which only came later, as the real path to righteousness.

CHAPTER 11

WHAT PAUL MEANT BY "ANAMNESIS"

To be clearer about what happens at daily celebrations of the Mass, the critical question becomes whether "anamnesis," the Greek word translated by general consent as "remembrance" or "memory" in the words of institution, can bear the construe of re-call, as opposed to a mere recall? Interestingly, it is only in 1 Corinthians and in Luke's gospel that the term "anamnesis" occurs at all in the context of the institution of the Mass. It is not present in that context in either Mark or Matthew or anywhere else in the New Testament. As to those two gospels, they only say: "Do this." With Luke, who does provide an amplification, the odds are that he derived it from Paul. Given that, everything depends on whether it is possible to find an internal clue that would point to Paul's intention in using the term. Did Paul simply intend by his term "anamnesis" a mere "memory," "commemoration," or "remembrance," or did he mean something much stronger? Did he mean "recall," or did he mean "re-call"?

The only verbal clue to his intention seems to be at 1 Corinthians 11:29–30, where Paul warned: "All who eat and drink without discerning the body, eat and drink judgment upon themselves. It is for this reason that many of you are ill and weak, and some have died." If, by "anamnesis," Paul were to have simply meant "remembrance" or such-like, and the Corinthian eucharistic gatherings were thus only for the purpose of remembering

Christ's death in our stead, then those who were disrespectful or skeptical at the memorial celebration would now only be skeptical or disrespectful about Christ's death in our stead. They might still be punished with sickness or death for their effrontery, but it would be incomprehensible and highly unlikely that the reason for their affliction would, by misdirection, turn out to be their epistemic failure to discern the body and blood of our Lord in the eucharistic bread and wine.

If, on the other hand, the purpose of the gatherings was actually to conduct a Mass in which the bread and wine become transformed as the flesh and blood of Christ, and was by no means simply a memorial, then Paul's admonition, that those who would attend such a eucharistic Mass ought to examine themselves and their beliefs before eating the consecrated bread and drinking the consecrated wine, would become extremely pertinent. To attend and actually to partake of either the consecrated bread or wine with this awareness that a transformation was intended, and yet to be without the essential conviction, or be deliberately rejecting the reality of the new ontic status of the species, would indeed be sacrilegious. At least, in the light of Paul's explanation and caution, it should no longer be said that those gatherings were simply commemorative, thereby turning the utterance of the words of institution into a mere formulaic ingredient in what would be a purely commemorative celebration.

If, however, the purpose of Paul's gatherings was actually to conduct a eucharistic Mass or join the Mass at the Last Supper, and not merely to reminisce about Jesus, what would the expression that professed to state that purpose, "*eis ten emen anamnesin*," now have to mean? At the very least, in light of the above discussion, it would have to mean something far stronger than the weak "in remembrance of me."

Rabban Gamaliel, at whose school Paul claimed he had been an accomplished student well above his peers, was the grandson of Rabban Hillel, at whose own school the study of the Greek language and ideas had been strongly promoted. Rabban Gamaliel shared his grandfather's educational outlook in his conduct of his own school. At Acts 21:37, when Paul was about to be led to the barracks by detaining troops, he turned toward the commander to ask whether he could say something to him. Seemingly startled, the commander replied, "Do you speak Greek?" Besides, Paul preached to Greeks and exchanged words with them in many Greek cities including Athens itself, and even commented on an inscription, undoubtedly written in Greek, "to an unknown god."

Now, consider the following suggestion that Paul was borrowing from the Platonic use of the same term "anamnesis." Those familiar with the context of that term will recall that Plato's doctrine of anamnesis was really a doctrine of *recognition* and not simply of *recollection*. Its point was not the mere remembering or recall now of forms that were previously known by us in our preincarnate existence in a world, all of whose objects were forms and nonphysical. Rather, its point was to explain, now that we are incarnate and endowed with a physical body in a world that is physical, and whose objects are not forms but empirical, how we could successfully discern, that is, *recognize* and *identify*, or in any sense know, any of its objects at all. The doctrine of anamnesis was Plato's attempt at an answer.

At this intermediate stage of his philosophical development, Plato contended that physical objects gain a nature that is knowable only by their participating in once familiar forms or by having once familiar forms in-fixed, inhering or embodied in them. We would be able to recognize and grasp those physical objects only if we were able to recognize in them the once familiar specific forms in which they now participated, since it was those forms that gave them a nature at all, and fixed that nature (doctrine of participation, methexis).

This participation caused the physical objects to imitate, reflect, and resemble their inhering forms, and this resemblance, when detected by us, brings back to our minds the specific inhering forms and thereby reveals to us how to identify the particular physical objects (doctrine of imitation, mimesis). Those forms in which they participated made the things what they are and fix their ontic nature, while their imitation of the now re-called forms made the physical objects discernible and identifiable by us. In a word, we recognize and identify physical objects by recognizing, through a recollection prompted by resemblance, itself caused by imitation, the forms in which they participate, those forms being already known to us in our preincarnate being, but currently temporarily out of mind due to our new and unaccustomed reliance on our bodies and physical senses for obtaining information about our present world. If we did not now recollect the forms and recognize them in their present physical embodiment, we would have no cognitive awareness at all of the objects in this physical world. Thus, the theory of participation and the theory of imitation are obviously not *alternative* theories of explanation, as is often claimed, but actually complementary theories in Plato; one is metaphysical, relating to the being of physical objects, and the other is epistemological, relating to the possibility of our knowing them.

Is it not all too likely that this was what Paul was exploiting? Paul's own anamnesis was not so much a remembrance as a *recognition*, a *discernment*, as he says, of the body and blood of the Lord in the eucharistic bread and wine. The consecrated bread and wine posed a dual problem of their new nature and of our ability to recognize that nature. In Plato's case, the physical object is given a nature by the form that now inheres in it. In Paul's case, the consecrated bread and wine have been given a nature possessing a new charism and power that inhere in them now.

In Plato's case, we are able to discern the physical object by recognizing the remembered form that now inheres in it. In Paul's case, the process of recognition would have to come about in a quite different manner. The original apostles that had been at the Last Supper grasped and recognized the body and blood of Jesus in the consecrated bread and wine not by sight or by taste or other physical sense, but through a praeter-sensory faculty, that of faith guided by Jesus's affirmation, which enabled them to discern in the consecrated bread and wine a new saving charism and power that otherwise belong exclusively to the body and blood of Jesus Christ. As soon as Jesus said the words of institution, the bread and wine that he would be offering underwent a discernible transformation, a transformation that gave them salvific power. It is through this very same faculty, that of faith, that we all must and do grasp, or, in Paul's diction, discern the body and blood of Christ in the bread and wine consecrated during a eucharistic Mass, upon the authorized utterance of the words of institution by an officiant standing in loco Christi. Unlike the case of Plato, it does not depend on remembrance or recollection at all. In the words of Hebrews, faith gives palpability to the things for which we hope, and renders evident things we do not actually perceive (11:1). In 1 Corinthians, Paul was only cautioning those whose faith or lack of it would not let them discern or recognize the saving power of the body and blood of Christ in the consecrated bread and wine to refrain from the reception of either, a caution appropriate in any age since the Last Supper itself.

It should seem now that the true meaning of the portion of the words of institution in 1 Corinthians: "*touto poieite eis ten emen anamnesin*" would be: "this do, in order to discern me," taking "eis" to be the "eis" of purpose. "This do" would then be an injunction to utter *with felicity* the transforming words of institution in their proper setting.

The nub is that those Corinthian eucharistic gatherings were not memorial gatherings, but gatherings whose aim was to reinvoke and bring into play that eucharistic Mass of the Last Supper wherein the bread and wine became for us the body and blood of Christ. Paul's anamnesis was a recognition, a discernment of the body and blood of Christ duly re-called and made real in the eucharistic bread and wine. The Corinthian Mass, like every other valid Mass, re-called and made present to participants the same body and blood of our Lord as was consumed at the Last Supper, by endowing the present bread and wine with the salvific power and efficacy of the actual body and blood of Christ. Cognizant participants discerned them in this way in the consecrated bread and wine, and with that consciousness consumed them. Those, then, who partake without thus discerning the body of Christ would have spurned the salvific offer of Jesus Christ, and would, ungraced, consequently be eating and drinking judgment against themselves (1 Corinthians 11:29).

A comparison is often made with the eating of the Passover lamb. The difference is in fact overwhelming. In the celebration of the Passover of the Lamb meal, participants are encouraged to project themselves into the Exodus itself. Remembering the Passover really is connecting within one's own consciousness a historic series of events with appreciation and gratitude for the past that has preserved oneself and an expectation and hope for a continued and future deliverance. Israelites were bidden to *remember* or bear in their individual consciousnesses the saving deeds of God throughout their generations, not merely *recollect* them at set times. The proper Greek term for this, favored in the Septuagint, was not anamnesis but mnemosunon as the rendering for the Hebrew *zikarron.*

On the other hand, Paul's term used in relation to the Mass is anamnesis not mnemosunon, and his term is appropriate for a discrete recollection, as opposed to say, a lingering remembrance of a highly cherished one. Properly understood, it relates to an acknowledging recollection, a discernment in this case, of what Christ said he was offering those present at the Last Supper: to eat and drink for the forgiveness of sins. Only Christ's body and blood possessed that salvific power, and neither can be duplicated or replicated, as the Passover lamb must be from year to year. At Mass, it is precisely Christ's very body and blood that are made available to communicants. This really is the crucial difference from Passover remembrances. Remembrance of Passover does not include a belief that it is the very lambs eaten on the eve of the Exodus that are being consumed at each and every subsequent Passover observance. Paul's anamnesis does involve an insistence that it is the very body and blood of Jesus Christ himself in which communicants partake. His anamnesis is not a historic projection and bonding, but a retroactive and actual participation in the original eucharistic meal.

Jesus's injunction that this be repeatedly done was his way of bringing within the ambit of the Last Supper all of us who had not been actually present, including all future generations, so that we might become, in effect, retroactively present at that Mass of the Last Supper, where Jesus was both the officiant and the victim. Each time the Mass has been said since the Last Supper, those attending have, in effect, called it back through the ordained, and thus empowered, officiant and entered that Mass with Christ freeing us from our sins (Revelations 5:8) by offering his person in our place (Isaiah 53:12). Blessed indeed are those who are called to that supper of the remission of sins. Every valid celebration of the Mass becomes a real bonding with, and vehicle into, that one Mass that is indeed timelessly recognized in heaven, and, through whose timeless reception there, Jesus can always be said to be interceding for us with the Father and be taking our sins upon himself, for what is historical on earth is timeless in heaven.

The historical expiatory death of Jesus on the cross meant neither that those born later were born too late, nor that the world subsequently has been without sin. In his first letter, the apostle John warned at 1:8–10 (NRSV): “If we say that we have no sin, we deceive ourselves, and the truth is not in us. If we confess our sins, he who is faithful and just will forgive us our sins, and cleanse us from all unrighteousness. If we say that we have not sinned, we make him a liar, and his word is not in us.” Indeed, Jesus’s declaration to Peter (Matthew 16:19 NRSV) “whatever you bind on earth will be bound in heaven, and whatever you loose on earth will be loosed in heaven,” to the church at large (18:17–18). “If the member refuses to listen to them, tell it to the church, and if the offender refuses to listen even to the church, let such a one be to you as a Gentile,” and to his disciples during his first postresurrection appearance to them (John 20:23) that whose sins they forgave, would be forgiven, and whose sins they retained, would be retained, clearly indicated that we would, unsurprisingly, continue to sin, and this is precisely why we needed Jesus to say, “Do this.”

In every valid celebration of the Mass, the duly ordained priest is fully empowered to beseech the Father to make the gifts on the altar become for us the body and blood of Jesus Christ, and so they do. They become endued with the power and efficacy of that very same body and blood of which those present at the Last Supper partook, not replicas, not duplicates, not any other substitute. What would be the source and power of a duplicate? What would be its point?

The upshot is that, in any age, communicants can in their own location partake of Jesus’s body and blood, just as if we ourselves had been present at the original Last Supper. After all, Jesus Christ offered himself as the bearer of the sins of the whole world once and for all in one, unrepeated, and unrepeatable sacrifice at the one Last Supper. That sacrifice was sufficient for its purpose, and did not stand in need of repetition, addenda, or supplement, because when Jesus on that occasion took over the sins of the whole world, the scope of that action included sins already committed as well as sins yet to be committed. In the action of the Last Supper, Jesus already had a place for absolutely every sin that was going to be forgiven and expiated, and each such sin entered its place as it was committed and perhaps confessed. They clearly include all sins that receive priestly absolution.

Accordingly, when, following Jesus's injunction to "do this," our priest officiates at a eucharistic Mass, and we believingly and discerningly eat the consecrated host and drink the consecrated wine, we retroactively and successfully participate in the Last Supper itself, and so get our sins retroactively transferred to their proper place in Jesus for expiation through his one crucifixion. It is indeed through this efficaciousness that the sufficiency of the action in the Last Supper is respected and acknowledged. What every valid celebration of the Mass achieves is to recall, no, to re-call, and bring back not simply to mind but efficaciously and in reality the one Mass of the Last Supper. "Do ***this***" is Jesus's authorization and guarantee of the efficaciousness of the re-call.

The alternative to this would present a frightening thought. If the transformation that occurs at a celebration of the Holy Mass were to be completely new, it would mean that, on our own initiative, we would be palming off our sins on Jesus, and be asking him to now remit and expiate them through an action distinct from and supernumerary to the actions undertaken in the Upper Room and on Golgotha. And yet any new conversion must provide its own mortal precrucifixion body, for only such a body could be sacrificed, given that the expiatory sacrifice must result in death. Since his resurrection, Jesus has possessed only a glorified resurrected body, over which death can have no dominion, and which consequently cannot possibly ever be sacrificed for either the remission of sins or their expiation. What would a body newly procured be, if it were to be distinct from the precrucifixion body of Jesus that was offered at the Last Supper to his apostles? This quandary is surely the alternative to bypassing the one Mass at the Last Supper and celebrating a new Mass or that Mass anew.

CHAPTER 12

WHY AND HOW THE MAN JESUS ROSE FROM THE DEAD

There still remained a danger for us, however. This danger lay in the finality of death as a liability from sin. It is this inner connection between sin and death that caused us, sinful as we are, to be incapable of self-salvation, incapable of expiating our own sins and thereafter living to tell the story. Our own death will neither obliterate nor expiate our sins, for that death is the outcome of our own sinfulness; it is something we suffer, something that happens to us, and not something we can do anything *with*. Our own death would only put a stop to our continued sinning. But Jesus's death, the death of a spotless victim, was able to expiate our sins because his death on the cross was not a consequence of his own sinfulness. It was designed as a sacrifice for the sins of others, so that we can die purged of our sins.

Now, if the man Jesus was saddled with the sins of the whole world when he was crucified, or, in Peter's previously quoted words, "He himself bore our sins in his body on the cross." (cf Isaiah 53:12; 1 Peter 2:21–24; also 1 John 2:2 and Hebrews 2:9), why and how was he able to overcome his own death and come back to life?

The answer is not that he was God, although that is not in dispute. In the "Hymn of Jesus" at Philippians 2:9–11, God bestowed on Jesus a name above every other name, such that at the invocation of Jesus by the name in question, every knee must bend in heaven, on earth, and under the earth. Now, what name could that have been, which would possess such magnitude of majesty and dignity? To be sure, that name could not have been "Jesus," for the name "Jesus" was common enough, first noted as belonging to Joshua, Moses's protégé and successor as leader of the Israelites (Exodus 17:9).

As a matter of fact, the only name known to us that possesses enough majesty to command such cosmic reverence is surely none other than that by which God himself was known, the tetragrammaton YHWH ("Yahweh"). This is without doubt the name the Father bestowed on the Son. Accordingly, that hymn to Jesus goes on to require every tongue to confess in consequence of Christ bearing the name in question that Jesus Christ is Lord up to the glory of the Father Himself ("eis" being taken in its limitative meaning of "up to"). Why else would every knee in heaven, on earth, and under the earth be required to bend at the invocation of the name, and do what is due only to God himself?

The glory that that name bestows is the glory that Jesus himself claimed to have had with the Father before the world began, and the glory, for whose restoration to the man Jesus, Jesus successfully asked at John 17:5, and the glory of God's name that Jesus confirms the Father has now restored to him (John 17:11). In his prologue to his gospel, the evangelist John commits to the same claim, when he writes in the Greek (Newadvent.org/bible, John 1:18), "θεὸν οὐδεις ἑώρακεν πώποτε: μονογενὴς θεὸς ὁ ὢν εἰς τὸν κόλπον τοῦ πατρὸς ἐκεῖνος ἐξηγήσατο," (No one has ever seen God but the only begotten who, by being in the Father's bosom, is God; *he* has given the account). The same point is affirmed at

Hebrews 1:8, relying on Psalm 45:6 (NRSV), where the Father addresses the Son as God. The Father says to the Son: "Your throne, O God, endures forever and ever. Your royal scepter is a scepter of equity." Indeed, in his final entry into Jerusalem, even the people, chanting under the force of inspiration, acknowledged Jesus's humanness by calling him the son of David and yet invoked his divinity by acclaiming him as coming with the name of the Lord—not in whose name, but in what name, with what title! It was clearly this understanding that caused the Jewish leaders to protest at that point that this was much too much.

Surely it is not by virtue of Jesus's being the second person of the Holy Trinity that he was able to rise from the dead, for in that light, he would not really have died (cp 1 Corinthians 15:21). And yet the man Jesus needed really to die under sentence of the sins of the whole world, that being a cup that could not possibly be set aside. The whole reason he became a little less than the angels in becoming human was so that he would be able to suffer death (Hebrews 2:9).

If, however, the man Jesus were to have stayed dead, he would have been in little position to offer anyone a credible means of salvation. His resurrection, on the other hand, would mean that death was unable to hold him: he would have destroyed the ostensible axiom that when you are *dead*, you *are* dead. He would have demonstrated once and for all that sin would not now inevitably lead to unending death in a human being, for he himself was a human being who had been laden with the sins of the world. In Jesus's resurrection, we all gained a sure means of salvation from the finality of death, because he, a human being, died while he was in full possession of our sins, expiated them in his death, and then rose from the dead. This is what Jesus came to earth to do: not simply to take away our sins, but to establish for us a clear path to salvation, a path to abundant life or life without end.

How, then, was the man Jesus able to rise from the dead? The answer is not that with his death he had fully expiated sin, and, being thereafter without sin, he would as a matter of course rise up. If this were so, would not all those, all of whose sins have been expiated through Jesus's death, when they themselves die, then experience a similar resurrection following their own death, having posthumously become sinless. No, we cannot claim that because Jesus's death expiated our sins, our death should with scant delay be followed by our own resurrection. That this does not happen would suggest that, even though our sins may be expiated when we die, there still is no autonomic process that would trigger a self-resurrection or end in one.

It would be even more preposterous to suppose, as some others of Paul's flock believed, that their own resurrection must have already occurred (2 Timothy 2:18), thinking of themselves as now being alive in a sinless state in consequence of the expiatory death of Jesus.

The death of Jesus is like no other, for his death was a sacrifice to expiate sin. No other death could do the same thing, for no other decedent would antecedently be without sin, so as to have become an acceptable sacrifice for sin. This means that we cannot expiate our own sins, let alone those of others by our dying. Consequently, until we have some clarity about the case of the man Jesus, we cannot even cite his resurrection as any sort of precedent for our own future.

Unlike any other human being, Jesus of Nazareth was without sins of his own. With the completion of his atoning self-sacrifice, the demands of God's justice were fully met. With the encumbrance of our sins now completely cast off from him, what was left of Jesus was a personally never-sinning man on whom, in consequence, death, as the wages of sin, never initially had any purchase, and so could not now have any possible purchase, for Jesus's assumption of our sins did not make him *personally sinful, only personally liable for the sins of others.* The man Jesus never had sins of his own that would need to be expiated through a death or that would lead to his own death. This, possibly, is why messianic lore held that the Messiah would never die once he appeared, for he always would be sinless.

Being without sin of his own, Jesus was never liable to die. He only became subject to death by acquiring our sins, even while still remaining personally without sin. Once Jesus had expiated our sins and cast them off, sin, and with it death, could no longer have any connection with him, for he was still personally without sin. In death, his body was not the body of a sinner as ours would constantly be. Always without sins of his own, he was always personally not subject to death. An innocent and utterly sinless person, his post-atonement persistence in death would be completely inexplicable and utterly without a basis. That is how Jesus had the power to take up his life again: "For this reason, the Father loves me, because I lay down my life so that I may take it up again. Nobody takes it away from me: but I lay it down myself. And I have the power to lay it down: and I have the power to take it up again" (John 10:17–18 NRSV). Besides, the Father, God, would surely never have had any demands on Jesus's person as such, and would therefore have no further interest in his death. Accordingly, God's justice too would not allow Jesus to remain in death (Psalm 16:10, Acts 2:24).

It is indeed extremely important not to see Jesus's resurrection as a discrete event. Paul seems to be the first person on record to have emphasized Christ's resurrection in the context of our salvation, for unless Paul was right, as he indeed was, Christ's resurrection would have had nothing to do with our own salvation, and would have been nothing but part of Christ's own exit strategy from the world, for once having died, he would need to rise again from the dead in order to leave this world.

Even at the ascension, it seems that the apostles still had not fully grasped the nature of Jesus's Messiahship. They were still pressing him on the matter of the restoration of the physical kingdom to the nation. "They asked him, 'Lord, is this the time when you will restore the kingdom to Israel?'" (Acts 1:6 NRSV). This political understanding of his Messiahship was largely responsible for their dispiritedness and pusillanimity at the seemingly all-ending crucifixion, as was confessed in the conversation on the way to Emmaus, and was clearly the cause of the disciples' going underground following the crucifixion. It was not until the manifestations at Pentecost that they would attain an adequate grasp of Jesus's Messiahship and the fullness of its power. Mark 9:10 reports that when Jesus asked the accompanying apostles at the Transfiguration not to mention what they had seen until after he had risen from the dead, they started asking one another what "rising from the dead" could mean, for if Jesus was really the Messiah they believed him to be, he should never die. Little wonder the resurrection was a complete surprise to all of them, and was greeted with incredulity.

This being so, it is hardly surprising that the consensus of scripture is that Jesus's resurrection from the dead was not so much a self-resurrection as an act of God the Father. To the apostles, God raised Jesus from the dead, and it is Jesus who in turn would raise his own redeemed from the dead (Matthew 16:21, 17:23; Luke 9:22; John 6:40, 6:44, 6:54; Acts 2:24, 4:10, 10:40, 13:30, 34, 37; 1 Corinthians 6:14, 15:15–16; 2 Corinthians 4:14; Ephesians 1:20; Colossians 2:12; 1 Thessalonians 1:10; Hebrews 11:19; Galatians 1:1; Romans 4:24–25, 6:4, 8:11, 10:9). Our own resurrection from death would be a free-will gift of Jesus, the original author of life. It is a transitive mystery, not an intransitive one.

During a eucharistic celebration, we partake of the body and blood of Christ. In so partaking, as suggested earlier, we subscribe to Jesus's new injunction. Our partaking of his body is much more than a simple continuation of extant Judaic tradition regarding the distribution of the body of a sacrificed victim among its beneficiaries. In partaking of the body of Christ, we are incorporating a living victim already sacrificed for the remission of our as yet unexpiated sins. It is this retroactive precrucifixion incorporation that enables us to be crucified with him by delegation, and, by delegation, rise with him on the third day to our own possibility of eternal life. It is this salvific incorporation that befalls us when we eat the flesh that Jesus was offering us in urging: "Do not work for the food that perishes, but for the food that endures for eternal life, which the Son of Man will give you. For it is on him that God the Father has set his seal" (John 6:27 NRSV). It was possibly this salvific fusion that Paul had in mind when he wrote: "Do you not know that all of us who have been baptized into Christ Jesus were baptized into his death? Therefore we have been buried with him by baptism into death, so that, just as Christ was raised from the dead by the glory of the Father, so we too might walk in newness of life. For if we have been united with him in a death like his, we will certainly be united with him in a resurrection like his" (Romans 6:3–6 NRSV).

There are two other institutional avenues whereby Jesus assumes our sins. One of these is the initiation rite of baptism. Through baptism, historical sins are washed away from us and retroactively transferred to Jesus for inclusion in his expiatory act on the cross. Since the sacrament of baptism is unrepeatable, subsequent sins cannot be washed away in the same manner, but can still be retroactively transferred to Jesus through the institution of the Mass and the rite of confession and priestly absolution. Furthermore, God is not restricted by institutions, and Jesus Christ is able to dispense his grace to whomever he pleases, wherever and whenever he chooses. By such dispensations, sins are noninstitutionally forgiven, but are forgiven nonetheless, through their incorporation into Jesus's one assumptive act to which there is no alternative, and atoned for through his one expiatory act from which there is no divergence. All in all, it is in Christ that God has forgiven us, there being "no other name under heaven given among mortals, by which we must be saved" (Acts 4:12 NRSV). In truth, no one can come to the Father except through Christ, for no one who does not have the grace of everlasting life in himself or herself can come to the Father. Jesus Christ alone does. He is the Life eternal (1 John 5:20), and thus Jesus Christ becomes the Way (John 14:6) to the Father.

Two ancillary questions remain. The first question is why we still die, if, as John has it at 1 John 3:14, we have passed from death to life. Part of the answer could surely be that our earthly bodies are biological entities that age and decay, or, as Paul has it, they are corruptible. Now, nothing corruptible can enter into the presence of God, who is eternal. In order to enter God's presence, it is necessary for us to vacate our corruptible, mortal bodies for incorruptible, everlasting ones. Vacating our corruptible bodies is all that is now left of death. The resurrection of the body is the reconfiguration of presently corruptible bodies as new incorruptible ones, the bodies in which we reemerge in the transition to our new life after our death.

The second question is this: if we died with Jesus on the cross, what are we still doing here? We certainly have not already resurrected. The temporal society in which we now live is a civil society, but the society that God is re-creating for us is not a civil society: it is a communion of saints. In our civil society, large segments of the population are fully accepted as autonomous adults, empowered to arrange and conduct their own affairs and lives according to their own lights. Our experience in civil society is a salient modifier of our present intuitions, ideals, common sense, and the persuasiveness of social and normative arguments. The contrast between the ways of civil society and the ways of the communion of saints can be illustrated from the Hebrew Bible and the New Testament.

When the Israelites were suffering from extreme thirst, God asked Moses to command the rock to yield its waters. To human reason, sharpened by its experience of causality in civil society, it seemed preposterous to address a rock as a way of getting it to yield its water, instead of simply whacking it. Moses remembered that earlier on he had been commanded to *strike* the rock at Horeb to release its waters, not *address* it. He had done so before with success, and had named the place Massah and Meribah (Exodus 17:6–7). This time, however, following his own reasoning based on his earlier experience, for good measure he whacked the present rock not once but twice (Numbers 20:1–13)! Moses did not on the present occasion draw upon his faith, whose hallmark is obedience, even though he had not too long ago displayed both faith and obedience in his powerful encounters with Pharaoh and in the magnificent parting of the Yam Suph, the Sea of Reeds.

Standing in sharp contrast with this is Abraham, who had abruptly uprooted himself from his native land at God's earlier request, and was now being asked by the same God to raise his knife to his son, Isaac, when God asked for Abraham's only promised son as a holocaust. Abraham's utter obedience and unwavering trust in God contrary to all common sense became construed as his righteousness. That demand was flabbergasting, for the same God had promised that that same Isaac born of Sarah, not of a different woman, would be at the head of a line through which Abraham would become the father of many nations, Jew and Gentile alike. If Abraham was now to slay as a sacrifice Isaac, who at this point had no progeny of his own, would it not stand to human reason and logic that God's promise to Abraham could no longer be kept? Indeed, Abraham himself would have had a hand in dashing his own hopes. The true measure of his faith was that he abandoned his human logic and reason and, fully trusting in God, left it to God to unravel his own conundrum.

At Matthew 16:13–23, Jesus had just blessed Simon Peter for the Father's revelation to him that Jesus himself was indeed the Christ, the Son of the living God. In appreciation, Jesus promptly appointed Peter holder of the keys to the kingdom of heaven. However, when Jesus went on to divulge his forthcoming passion and crucifixion, naturally Peter would not hear of it. Of course, "no such thing shall ever happen to you," Peter declared. Jesus must at all costs do the sensible thing and stay away from Jerusalem. This commonsensical gem only earned Peter a rebuke and the opprobrium of thinking as humans think, not as God does. In his counsel, Peter was following modes of thought that would surely be laudable in civil society, rather than ones distinctive of the communion of saints. Jesus's rebuke highlights the difference between right-thinking in civil society and right-thinking in the communion of saints, whose denizens are even expected to forgive their offenders not seventy-seven times, but times without number.

The reason is that God is love, and the manifestation of love toward those who sin is mercy. Because we ourselves are created in the image of God, we are created to love, and the manifestation of love toward those who err against us is forgiveness. Since loving is the *essence* of God, forgiveness, as an expression of our loving nature, must know no numerical bounds.

In the presently unfinished communion of saints, relatively few of us have reached adulthood, and most of us are at different stages of our tutelage. As Paul colorfully put it, generally we are in our green and salad days. We are engaged on a journey of instruction, practice, and habituation. This journey is taking place within the context of civil society, for which the developing communion of saints serves as leavening. We already know some of the loving behavior that should distinguish us while we continue within our civil society habitat. Turn the other cheek; do not judge others; give your cloak away to those who ask; return good for evil; do not get even but forgive one another, so that the Father may forgive us (Matthew 6:14–15); do not lay up treasure on earth—none of them intrinsic to civil society, yet every one of them ennobling it. We are to do good without ceasing.

The basic relations that are characteristic of civil society are founded on principles of commerce or the commingling of private interests, while the basic relations energizing the communion of saints are based on principles of love. Plato once toyed with the notion that the enacting of statute law was pointless, as good people would not need it, and evil people would not heed it. Aristotle, for his part, knew that people became good through the practice of goodness and through habituation formed by repeated exercise.

In our own tutelage toward adulthood in the communion of saints, we have but two principles to heed, to guide, and to inform our manner of being, our interrelations, and our deeds. At this stage in our growth, we know these principles in the form of two commandments derived from Torah (Deuteronomy 6:5, Leviticus 19:18, but also Mark 12:30–31, Matthew 22:37–38, and Luke 10:27); first, that we shall love the Lord our God with all our heart, and with all our soul, and with all our mind, and with all our strength, and, second, that we shall love our neighbor as ourselves. After we have reached adulthood in the communion of saints, we shall no longer know these as commandments; instead, they will present to us as inward expressions of our own autonomy and maturity.

In very few of us has living according to such principles become second nature. In fact, in two things only does God follow our lead: if we give our children bread and not a stone, fish and not a snake when they ask, God will likewise give us good things when we ask (Matthew 7:7–11), and if we forgive others, then God will likewise forgive us (Matthew 6:15). Indeed, the heavenly Father will make us pay back our whole debt, unless we forgive others from our heart (Matthew 18:35). Meanwhile, we continue to be on earth in order to advance our tutelage. In the words of Jesus, who taught us by saving precept and divine example: "Be holy as your Father in heaven is holy." The practice of love, as enjoined above, is in all truth nothing less than the practice of holiness itself.

Printed in the United States
By Bookmasters